English to get on with

A situational, structured approach
to phrasal/prepositional verbs

ANN BAKER

HEINEMANN EDUCATIONAL BOOKS
LONDON

Heinemann Educational Books Ltd
22 Bedford Square, London WC1B 3HH

LONDON EDINBURGH MELBOURNE AUCKLAND
HONG KONG SINGAPORE KUALA LUMPUR NEW DELHI
NAIROBI JOHANNESBURG IBADAN KINGSTON
EXETER (NH) PORT OF SPAIN

ISBN 0 435 28105 4

Printed in Great Britain by
Richard Clay (The Chaucer Press) Ltd
Bungay, Suffolk

Contents

Teacher's introduction *1*

Introductory unit *8*

Unit 1 to go   Pattern 1 Verbs *13*

Unit 2 to go   Pattern 2 Verbs *19*

Unit 3 to put   Pattern 3 Verbs *25*

Unit 4 to make   Pattern 2 and 3 Verbs *30*

Unit 5 to come   Pattern 1 and 2 Verbs *36*

Unit 6 to call   Passivization *42*

Review—Units   1-6 'Wh' Questions Quiz *48*

Unit 7 to run   Passivization *49*

Unit 8 to turn   Passivization *55*

Unit 9 to break   Object Pronoun Variations *61*

Unit 10 to get   Pattern 2 (ii) Verbs *66*

Unit 11 to look   Pattern 2 (ii) Verbs *72*

Unit 12 to take   Object Pronoun Variations *78*

Review—Units   7-12 'Wh' Questions Quiz *84*

Unit 13 Review   Gerund structures *85*

Answers to quiz questions *91*

Acknowledgements

The author wishes to thank the following:
Joe de Freitas, for arousing my interest in this subject; Roland Hindmarsh, for his encouragement and time spent discussing the book; teachers of the British Council Centre, Tehran who helped try out the material, particularly those who allowed me to observe their classes in action.

Teacher's Introduction

AIMS

Phrasal and Prepositional Verbs usually form a fairly small part of most English courses, and an extremely large part of conversational English. Consequently, students of English as a foreign language are often confused and frustrated when they cannot understand this kind of everyday conversation:

'I ran into Mary the other day.'
'Oh, yes. Tom's fiancée. They were always falling out, and he broke it off in the end.'
'He told me he couldn't put up with her mother.'

And it is no wonder that they often feel that they are not making any progress in the 'real', as opposed to the 'classroom' English.

English to Get on With is designed to bridge this gap by providing teachers of Intermediate students with material for teaching and practising these expressions. It can also be used by students studying alone, and students who have reached the level required towards the end of book two of most basic course books should be able to handle the structures and vocabulary involved. It is written for adults, and would also be suitable for mature secondary school students.

SIMPLIFIED TERMINOLOGY

Teachers as well as students are often confused when they try to study this aspect of the language, because there is much disagreement over what to call these expressions. In this book a simplified terminology has been adopted:

1

Examples	Simplified Terms	Linguistic Terms
Tom and Mary *fell out*.	Pattern 1 Verb	Phrasal Verb without Object OR Intransitive Verb + Adverb Combination
I *ran into* Mary. I *ran into* her.	Pattern 2 Verb	Prepositional Verb OR Verb+Preposition Combination
He couldn't *put up with* her mother. He couldn't *put up with* her.	Pattern 2(ii) Verb	Prepositional-Phrasal Verb OR Verb + Adverb + Preposition Combination
Who *broke off* the engagement? Who *broke* the engagement *off*? Who *broke* it *off*?	Pattern 3 Verb	Phrasal Verb OR Verb + Adverb Combination

This simplified terminology is useful because it helps students to remember the patterns these verbs follow with nouns and pronouns. As in the examples above, there is one way of saying a Pattern 1 Verb, there are two ways of saying Pattern 2 Verbs, and there are three ways of saying Pattern 3 Verbs.

PROBLEMS FOR THE LEARNER

In trying to master these expressions, students are confronted by four problems:
1 semantics - understanding what the expressions mean.
2 structure - knowing what patterns the expressions can follow.
3 phonology - producing correct, natural stress.
4 collocation - knowing with which particular groups of words the expressions can be used.
The material in this book is presented with these problems in mind.

1 Understanding: Each lesson unit introduces the expressions to be learnt in the context of part of a serial story. This assists comprehension as well as motivation, for students are not required to deal with new characters, new themes, or extensive new vocabulary in each unit.

The questions on the introductory reading passages are designed to assist comprehension rather than to test it. For example: Unit 1, Question 1. When did Fred's alarm clock *ring*?

It went . . . . . . at eight o'clock. (line 1).

The student is asked merely to complete the answer by referring to the line indicated in the passage. If he has not understood the meaning of the expression from the context of the story, he can refer to the words in italics in the question, which give an explanation of it. The meaning that is given here may of course be expanded later in the unit. For example, in Unit 1, Exercise 1 he will find that 'to go off' can be used in other contexts, such as, 'The bomb went off.'

2 Structural Patterns: Each unit deals with common expressions found with a particular verb. Not only do students find satisfaction in learning the subject in this methodical way, but also this approach lends itself to structuring of the material, as certain verbs tend to follow particular patterns. For example, by teaching expressions with the verb 'to go' in Units 1 and 2, only Pattern 1 and 2 Verbs are introduced, as this verb has no expressions which follow Pattern 3. Then in Unit 3 the third pattern is introduced with the verb 'to put'.

In each reading passage the expressions to be learnt are numbered to show which pattern they follow. The advantage of this will not be immediately obvious in the first three units as each pattern is introduced separately, but here students will become familiar with the numbers, and in later units they will find this very useful. For example, normally in first reading, 'She broke off the engagement,' the student has no way of knowing whether he can say, 'She broke off it,' or, 'She broke it off'. But here - 'She [3]broke off the engagement' - the number tells him immediately.

The introductory Unit presents the three basic patterns, here using only simple, non-idiomatic expressions. In the following units each of these patterns is practised first separately, then contrastively, before further aspects such as passivization and object pronoun variations are introduced. The final unit is a review of verbs already learnt with gerund constructions. Two further reviews are given after Units 6 and 12 in the form of a short Quiz. These revise the expressions learnt in the preceding units, and also give practice in 'wh' question forms. They can be used for class competitions with the students in one team putting the questions to the other team, with points awarded for each correct answer.

Extensive practice is given in structural patterns in the Exercises following each reading passage.

3 Stress: The following patterns are introduced:

Pattern 1 Verbs: The alarm clock went OFF.

Pattern 2 Verbs: The dog WENT for MARY.
                        The dog WENT for her.

Pattern 2(ii) Verbs: He went IN for TENNIS.
                        He went IN for it.

Pattern 3 Verbs: We put up some FRIENDS.
                        We put some FRIENDS up.
                        We put them UP.

This is of course an over-simplification of the many complicated stress variations possible with these verbs, particularly with Pattern 2. Teachers must keep in mind that these are merely guidelines, without which Intermediate students tend to produce arbitrary and often unnatural stress such as:

The dog went FOR her.
The alarm clock WENT off.
He went in FOR tennis.
We PUT THEM up.

Mistakes like these not only sound unnatural, but also often lead to misunderstanding of the speaker's meaning. For these reasons the items in the Exercises are grouped according to structural patterns, and before each group Stress Practice is given in which students listen and repeat in order to establish the stress patterns to be used in the subsequent exercises.

4 Collocation: The danger of giving students mere lists of meanings for these expressions, is that they consequently try to use them in conjunction with words which do not fit. For example, if a student learns that 'to go in for' means 'to do something in your spare time', he may produce sentences like this:

I go in for washing dishes.
I go in for doing my homework.

Or he may produce a sentence like:

I went in for tennis yesterday.

To avoid these errors he must meet the expression in context, and practise it thoroughly to establish it as something automatically linked with the words which normally surround it and the verb tenses with which it is normally used.

In the Exercises students are given this kind of practice in the form of drills, substitution tables and dialogues. It is generally not a good idea for the teacher to ask students to try to think of other examples than those given, and students would be wise, until a much more advanced level than this book aims at, to use the expression only in the type of sentences practised.

SYLLABUS ALLOTMENTS

The material in this book has been tested and found successful with pre-First Certificate in English, and pre-Certificate of Proficiency in English classes, each unit taking approximately 60, 45 and 30 minutes of class time respectively, excluding written Tests. At any of these levels teachers may wish to allot the material to cover one or more terms to fit in with syllabus requirements. The following are suggested syllabus allotments to cover various types of courses:

1-Term Course: approximately one lesson per week, or in teaching blocks:

	i.	Introductory Unit + Units 1-4
	ii.	Units 5-9
	iii.	Units 10-13
2-Term Course:	Term 1	Introductory Unit + Units 1-6
	Term 2	Units 7-13
1-Year Course:	Term 1	Introductory Unit + Units 1-4
	Term 2	Units 5-9
	Term 3	Units 10-13
2-Year Course:	Year 1	Term 1 Introductory Unit
		Term 2 Units 1-3
		Term 3 Units 4-6
	Year 2	Term 1 Units 7-9
		Term 2 Units 10-11
		Term 3 Units 12-13

These allocations allow for the most convenient breaks in the serial story, which has been written so that students who begin in the second year of a two year course will be able to follow it successfully. A student starting late in any course should read the Introductory Unit, in order to understand the numbering system used.

SUGGESTED LESSON PLAN

1 Briefly introduce the pattern(s) to be taught. This can be done with the help of the example and picture at the beginning of each unit.
2 (students' books closed) Students listen to the story.
3 (students' books closed) Students answer the questions orally, giving short answers only. Students should not be expected to use the Pattern Verb responses at this stage.
4 (students' books closed as much as possible) Exercises: students benefit most from an oral approach to this section, keeping their books closed for as long as they can. The exercises have been arranged so that this session can start off as purely oral work.
5 Students read the story at the beginning of the unit, and complete the answers to the questions.
6 The test can be given to the whole class orally, or students can be asked to produce written answers either in groups or individually. It

5

can be very usefully prepared as homework to be discussed in the next lesson.

Alternatively, students can read the story before doing the Exercises, reversing the order of steps four and five. The plan suggested above has the advantage of giving students practice in first listening and speaking, and then reading and writing, so that the last two activities are reinforcement of what they have already learnt orally.

SUGGESTIONS FOR USING THE EXERCISES

1 Drills: These are recognizable by the headings, *cue: response:* and should be done as far as possible with students' books closed. It is best for the students to repeat the first response after the teacher. Then the cues can be given by the teacher, and the students give the responses either individually or in groups.

Some are dialogue drills. For example:

Cue tennis
Response A: Do you go in for tennis?

B: Yes, I do.
No, I don't.

At first the teacher may give A as the cue, so that students can practise B's answer. After this initial practice the teacher can merely give the cue word, and two students give the response in a simulated dialogue:

Teacher: tennis . . . . . . A (pointing to one student) . . . . . .
B (pointing to another student)
Student A: Do you go in for tennis?
Student B: Yes, I do.

2 Dialogues: Students usually need to read these, as they are longer or more complicated than the dialogue drills. They can be practised first chorally with the class repeating after the teacher, then in group work. The dialogues usually allow for practice in pairs, but where larger groups are needed this is indicated.

Substitution dialogues are also used. For example:

A Jim always **(x)** *arrives late for work.*
B Doesn't he get into trouble?
A No, he doesn't. He always gets away with it.

(x) arrives late for class
parks his car illegally
travels without a ticket

The words in italics following **(x)** in the dialogue can be replaced by those in the list **(x)**. It is best to do a few examples with the whole class first before starting group work, to ensure that students understand this procedure. With a more advanced class these may be used as dialogue drills, with the students' books closed, and the teacher giving

6

merely the italicized words as the cue.

3 Substitution Tables: Check that students know how to use these—that they can read across the dotted vertical lines, but not the horizontal lines. It is best to let the students first study the table and ask questions about any unfamiliar vocabulary before being asked to read or write sentences from it.

Introductory Unit

This book teaches you how to use expressions in which verbs are combined with such words as: in, out, on, off, into, along, at, with, etc. These words are easily understood in sentences like:

She's *on* the escalator.
They're going *into* the underground.

But expressions like:

I give *up*.
It's getting me *down*.
He got *out of* the work.
She came *into* a lot of money.

are more difficult to understand and use. As you know, expressions like these are used a lot, particularly in conversational English.

These expressions follow different patterns, and in this book the patterns are numbered to help you to learn them more easily. Look at the examples in this story:

A lot of people were ²*going into* the underground station. Mrs Smith was ²*going down* the escalator when she suddenly remembered that she hadn't ³*switched off* her iron. She was very worried, but she had to ¹*go on* because she couldn't ¹*turn back*.

What do these numbers mean?
'1' means that this is a Pattern 1 Verb.
   Example: She couldn't ¹*turn back*.
   There is only *one* way of saying this verb.

'2' means that this is a Pattern 2 Verb.
   Example: She was ²*going down* the escalator.
              She was *going down* it.
   There are *two* ways of saying this verb.
   Pattern 2 Verbs sometimes have two words connected to the verb.
   Example: People were ²*coming out of* the station.
              People were *coming out of* it.

'3' means that this is a Pattern 3 Verb.
   Example: She hadn't ³*switched off* her iron.
              She hadn't *switched* her iron *off*.
              She hadn't *switched* it *off*.
   There are *three* ways of saying this verb.

Now read the rest of the story. How many ways can you say each of the verbs numbered in it?

When Mrs Smith ²*came out of* the station she ²*ran along* the street very fast, but she ¹*fell down* just outside her office. She ¹*got up* quickly, ²*went into* the office, and ¹*sat down*. ³*Taking off* her gloves, she ³*picked up* a telephone.

'You can ²*get into* the flat if you ²*climb up* a ladder,' she told her neighbour.

Ten minutes later the neighbour ¹*phoned back*.

'You had ³*switched* the iron *off*,' she told Mrs Smith, 'but you had forgotten to ³*turn off* the tap.'

EXERCISES

1 PATTERN 1 VERBS
Complete these sentences from the story.
The first one has been done for you as an example.

  a. Mrs Smith had to go on.
  b. She couldn't turn . . . . . .
  c. Mrs Smith fell . . . . . .
  d. She got . . . . . . quickly.
  e. The neighbour phoned . . . . . .

2 PATTERN 2 VERBS

Complete these pairs of sentences from the story.
The first one has been done for you as an example.

a. People were going into the station.
   People were going into it.
b. Mrs Smith ran along . . . .
   Mrs Smith ran along . . . .
c. She came . . . . the station.
   She came . . . .
d. 'You can get . . . . ,' she said.
   'You can get . . . . ,' she said.
e. 'Climb . . . . ,' she said.
   'Climb . . . . ,' she said.

3 PATTERN 3 VERBS

Complete these sentences from the story.
The first one has been done for you as an example.

a. Mrs Smith phoned up her neighbour.
   Mrs Smith phoned her neighbour up.
   Mrs Smith phoned her up.
b. She asked her to switch . . . . . . the iron.
   She asked her to switch the iron . . . . . .
   She asked her to switch it . . . . . .
c. Mrs Smith picked . . . . . . a telephone.
   Mrs Smith picked . . . .
   Mrs Smith picked . . . .
d. She took . . . . her gloves.
   She took . . . .
   She took . . . .
e. You had forgotten to turn . . . .
   You had forgotten to turn . . . .
   You had forgotten to turn . . . .

4 *Cue:*   *Response:*

Run along that wall.   You run along it first!
Run along that line.
Climb up that ladder.
Go into that room.
Walk along that street.
Climb up that rope.
Get into that car.
Go down these stairs.

5 *Cue:*   *Response:*

Switch off the lights.   You switch them off!

Switch off the TV.
Turn off the tap.
Phone up Mr Brown.
Pick up these books.
Take off your shoes.
Phone up your grandmother.
Pick up that pen.

6 *Cue:*   *Response:*
  Sit down.   I don't want to sit down.
  Climb up that tree.   I don't want to climb up it.
  Switch off the radio.   I don't want to switch it off.
  Take off your shoes.
  Go into that old house.
  Phone up Mrs Robinson.
  Walk along that wall.
  Fall down.
  Get up.
  Climb up that mountain.
  Pick up these shoes.
  Get into that car.
  Lie down.
  Switch off the lights.

TEST

A Fill in the spaces in this story:
When I got home I found I had forgotten my key and I couldn't
get . . . . . . the house. I sat . . . . . . and wondered what to do. Instead
of phoning . . . . . . my brother at his office, I stupidly decided to
climb . . . . . . the tree and get . . . . . . the house through an upstairs
window. So I took . . . . . . my coat and started climbing. I soon
decided that it was much too difficult, but I had to go . . . . . .   I had
almost reached the window when I fell . . . . . .

B Replace the words in italics by the words in brackets.
Example i: I went into *the library*. (it)
Answer: I went into it.
Example ii: I phoned up *my friend*. (her)
Answer: I phoned her up.

1 I phoned up *my brother*. (him)
2 Did you switch off *the lights*? (them)
3 They ran along *the wall*. (it)
4 We climbed up *the rope*. (it)
5 You should put *your shoes* on. (them)

C Use the verbs you practised in this unit to make a remark that could follow each of these in a conversation.

Example: How did you cut yourself? (down)

Possible Answers: I fell down.

I was climbing up a ladder and I fell down.

etc.

1 Aren't you tired of watching TV? (off)
2 Why do you want Mary's phone number? (up)
3 I'm too hot with this coat on. (off)
4 I'm tired of standing up. (down)
5 I can't finish this test. I've dropped my pen on the floor. (up)

Unit 1 – to go

His alarm clock ¹went off.

FRED AND MONICA

Fred's alarm clock ¹went off at eight o'clock, but he didn't get up. He turned over and thought about Monica. They had had an argument last night – about nothing, as usual.

Fred and Monica had been friends for a long time now. They never 5 talked about getting married, but Fred knew that this was what Monica wanted – and he was terrified.

'I couldn't get married,' he thought. 'I'm too young. I'm too poor. Prices are ¹going up all the time and my work at the office isn't ¹going ahead at all. No. I really can't afford to get married. Children! Well, 10 there just wouldn't be enough food to ¹go round. We'd all starve.' Fred's thoughts ¹went on.

Then seeing how late it was, Fred quickly got up and got dressed. He was just leaving for the office when the telephone rang. It was Monica!

15 'Fred!' she exclaimed, 'I couldn't sleep all night thinking about us. I just have to speak to you! And I must ask you now: Fred, when are we . . . . . . ?'

'I say, Monica,' said Fred very quickly, 'I'm just ¹going out. And . . . . er . . . . I forgot to tell you last night, I have to ¹go away for a

20 few days . . . . er . . . . on a business trip. So I must hurry. See you
soon, darling, I'll write to you of course. Bye!'

QUESTIONS

Complete the answers. Use the words from the story.

1 What time did Fred's alarm clock *ring*?
  It went . . . . . . at eight o'clock. (line 1)
2 Did Fred think that prices were *getting higher* or lower?
  He thought that prices were going . . . . . . (line 8)
3 Did Fred think his work at the office was *progressing* well?
  No. He thought his work wasn't going . . . . . . at all. (line 8)
4 Did he think that if he and Monica had some children, there would
  be *enough* food *for everyone*?
  No. He thought there wouldn't be enough food to go . . . . . (line 10)
5 How long did Fred's thoughts about this *continue*?
  His thoughts went . . . . . . until he saw how late it was. (line 11)
6 Was Fred telling the truth when he said that he was just *leaving the
  house*?
  Yes. He was just going . . . . . . when the telephone rang. (line 18)
7 Was Fred telling the truth when he said he had to *go on a trip* for a
  few days?
  No. He was telling a lie when he said he had to go . . . . . . (line 19)

14

EXERCISES

1 STRESS PRACTICE

Listen and repeat:
I'm just going OUT.
Prices are going UP.
I have to go AWAY.
Fred's thoughts went ON.
The alarm clock went OFF.
There wouldn't be enough to go ROUND.

2 GO ON

Example: Fred's thoughts *went on.*

Cue: Did you stop reading at the beginning of this page?
Response: No. I went on.

Now give the responses to the following cues.

Did the taxi driver stop when the lights turned red?
Did Mary stop singing when they threw tomatoes at her?
Did the children stop shouting when you asked them to?
Do you usually stop speaking in the middle of a sentence?
Does your teacher stop teaching in the middle of a lesson?
Do you stop answering in the middle of a drill?
Will you stop answering in the middle of this drill?
Will the party finish at eleven o'clock?
Will the party finish if the neighbours complain?

3 GO AWAY

Example: 'I have to *go away* for a few days.' said Fred.

Cue: on a business trip
Response: Mr Smith has gone away *on a business trip.*

Now give the responses to the following cues.

on holiday	on business
for a fortnight	for the weekend
for a few days	with his secretary
with his family	for ever

4 GO ROUND

Example: 'There wouldn't be enough food to *go round*.' Fred
thought.

i.
Cue: meat
Response: Is there enough *meat* to go round?

Cue: *knives*
Response: Are there enough *knives* to go round?

Now give the responses to the following cues.

bread	pencils
milk	paper
plates	books
butter	chairs

ii.

DIALOGUE PRACTICE:

A: Some more guests have arrived.
B: Heavens! Is there enough (**x**) *soup* to go round?
A: No. But we'll add some water to make it go round.

(**x**) **Substitute:** milk; stew; wine; whiskey.

5 GO OFF

Example: Fred's alarm clock *went off* at eight o'clock.

A gun, a bomb, a burglar alarm and a fire alarm can also go off.
These things are all specially prepared to make a loud noise.

Finish these sentences about them using the verb 'to go off':

When the thieves broke the window . . . . . .
I was cleaning the gun, and suddenly . . . . . .
Hundreds of people will be killed when . . . . . .
Everybody has run out of the building because . . . . . .

6 GO AHEAD

Example: 'My work at the office isn't *going ahead* at all,' thought Fred.

Make sentences from this table:

My work		very quickly.
Our English class	isn't going ahead	as well as we hoped.
That new road		at all.
Our new house		
This business		very slowly.
Our town	is going ahead	quickly.
This country		surprisingly well.

Example: My work is going ahead surprisingly well.

16

7 GO UP/DOWN

Example: 'Prices are *going up* all the time,' thought Fred.

This chart gives you some information about a cigarette factory:

	last year	this year	next year
cost of making cigarettes			
price of cigarettes			
number of cigarettes produced			
workers' wages			
profits			

Example: Last year the cost of making cigarettes *went up*.
This year the cost of making cigarettes *has gone down*.
Next year the cost of making cigarettes *won't go up or down*.

Make up sentences, following the example.

8 GO OUT

Example: Fred was just *going out* when the telephone rang.

DIALOGUE PRACTICE:

A: Hello. Can I speak to Mary, please?

B: I'm sorry. She's just gone out.

A: Has she gone out to the pictures?
theatre?

B: No. I think she went out to a party.
a dance.
an evening class.

TEST

A Fill in the spaces in this story:

It was breakfast time in the Blue Sky Cafe. The *egg timer went

. . . . . . and the cook took two *soft boiled eggs out of the pot. Business hadn't been going . . . . . . very well lately. The manager even made the cook add water to the soup if there wasn't enough to go . . . . . . The customers were always complaining because the prices kept going . . . . . . As a result, of course, the profits were going . . . . . . and so were the cook's wages. While the cook was thinking about all this, she dropped the eggs on the floor.

'That finishes it!' she exclaimed. 'I'm going to go . . . . . . and breathe some fresh air and smoke a cigarette.'

The waitress looked very worried. 'Don't worry,' the cook said to her. 'I won't go . . . . . . for ever. You won't have to cook the lunch!'

* egg timer: this is set to ring when the egg is cooked;
* soft-boiled egg: an egg that is boiled for a very short time.

B Use one of the verbs you practised in this unit to make a remark that could follow each of these in a conversation:
Example: They haven't finished building your new house yet.
Possible Answers: No. It isn't going ahead very quickly.
They've nearly finished. It's going ahead quite well.
etc.

1 I haven't seen the neighbours for a few days. Where are they?
2 Why are you leaving your job?
3 I've invited ten more people for dinner tonight, darling. Is that all right?
4 Why is this tea more expensive than it was last week?
5 Why are you late for class? Haven't you got an alarm clock?

Unit 2 – to go

George ²went in for hunting.   His dog ²went for Monica.
George went in for it.   His dog went for her.

The story so far: Fred knows that his girlfriend, Monica, wants to get married, so when she phones him up he tells her he is going away on a business trip. A few days later they see each other again at George's party.

GEORGE'S PARTY

Fred didn't enjoy George's party, and he drank too much. He was very nervous all evening, for he felt sure that Monica would speak to him again.
    The party was very successful. George ²went in for hunting, and
5 later in the evening he had a shooting competition for his guests. Everyone except Fred ²went in for it. Monica had never used a gun before, but she hoped that she would win a prize. She was very excited about it and she shouted so loudly that one of George's dogs ²went for her. It didn't bite her, but she cried a lot and asked Fred to take her
10 home.

Fred really shouldn't have drunk so much, for on the way home they talked about getting married, and in the end he ²went along with her suggestion that they should get engaged.

15 The next morning Fred woke up with a terrible hangover and remembered what had happened. He ²went without food all day and lay in bed ²going over his plan to escape.

'I could go away for a few days and just never come back,' he thought. This was his plan, but would he ever ²go through with it? Fred ²went through hours of worry as he lay in bed thinking. He had made a

20 promise, and he knew that he shouldn't ²go back on it.

QUESTIONS

Complete the answers. Use the words from the story.

1 What *hobby* did George *have?*
  He went . . . . hunting. (line 4)
2 Why didn't Fred *take part in* the shooting competition?
  He didn't go . . . . it because he was drunk. (line 6)
3 Who did George's dog *attack?*
  It went . . . . . . Monica. (line 8)
4 Fred *didn't like* Monica's suggestion, *but he agreed with it.* Why?
  He went . . . . her suggestion because he was drunk. (line 12)
5 Why did Fred *eat no* food all day?
  He went . . . . . . it because he was worrying. (line 15)
6 What plan was he *looking at and thinking about* as he lay in bed?
  He was going . . . . . . his plan to escape. (line 16)
7 Was Fred sure that he would *be brave enough to put his plan into action?*
  No. He wasn't sure that he would ever go . . . . it. (line 18)
8 Who *experienced* hours of worry?
  Fred went . . . . . . hours of worry. (line 19)
9 Did Fred think that he could make a promise and then *break it?*
  No. He knew that he shouldn't go . . . . his promise. (line 20)

EXERCISES

1 STRESS PRACTICE
  Listen and repeat:
  The dog WENT for MONICA.
  The dog WENT for her.
  He WENT without FOOD.
  He was GOING over his PLAN.

He WENT through HOURS of WORRY.

Note: Pattern 2 Verbs have a lot of variation in this stress pattern.

2 GO FOR
   Example: George's dog *went for* Monica.

   Cue: Mary
   Response:
   Student A: Mary mustn't touch that dog.
   Student B: Why not?
   Student A: It'll go for her.

   Now give the responses to the following cues.
   Susan   your friends
   Peter   we
   you   the children

3 GO THROUGH
   Example: Fred *went through* hours of worry.

   Cue: a bad time
   Response: I went through *a bad time* when I was ill.

   Now give the responses to the following cues.
   hours of pain   when I was in hospital
   weeks of worry   when I was in prison
   months of loneliness   when my best friend died
   a lot of difficulties   when I lost my job
   a bad time   waiting for the exam results

4 GO OVER
   Example: Fred lay in bed *going over* his plan to escape.

   Make sentences from this table:

I He She We They	went over had gone over 'll go over	the homework the composition the exercise it the letter the design the plan	several times. to check it. twice. again. to find any mistakes. very carefully.

Example: We went over it very carefully.

5 GO WITHOUT

Example: Fred *went without* food all day.

Complete these sentences with the clauses in B:

A. Their mother goes without food . . .
   I used to go without sleep . . .
   At the office we go without lunch . . .
   I'm going without sugar in my tea . . .
   We had to go without washing . . .
   There isn't any milk . . .

B. to save water.
   so we'll have to go without it.
   when I was preparing for exams.
   if we're too busy to eat it.
   because I'm getting too fat.
   if there isn't enough for the children.

6 STRESS PRACTICE

Listen and repeat:
He went IN for HUNTING.
He went IN for it.
He went ALONG with her SUGGESTION.
He went ALONG with it.
He shouldn't go BACK on his PROMISE.
He shouldn't go BACK on it.
Will he go THROUGH with his PLAN?
Will he go THROUGH with it?

7 GO ALONG WITH

Example: He *went along with* her suggestion.

Cue: idea
Response: Student A: I don't like his *idea*.
           Student B: Neither do I, but we'll go along with it.

Now give the responses to the following cues.
plan / ideas / plans / suggestions / proposal / suggestion

8 GO BACK ON

Example: He had made a promise, and he knew that he shouldn't
           go back on it.

Cue: a promise
Response: If you make *a promise* you shouldn't go back on it.

Now give responses to the following cues.
an agreement / mustn't / a promise / give a promise / give your word /
shouldn't / If I / If a gentleman

9 GO IN FOR
Example: George *goes in for* hunting.

DIALOGUE PRACTICE:
A: What hobbies do you go in for?
B: I go in for **(x)** *cards.*
C: Do you go in for **(y)** *chess* too?
B: No, I don't. But my neighbour / friend goes in for it.

(x) Substitute: tennis
collecting stamps
photography
skiing
dancing

(y) Substitute: table tennis
collecting coins
painting
mountaineering
acting

10 GO THROUGH WITH
Example: This was his plan, but would he ever *go through with* it?

DIALOGUE PRACTICE:
A: Why didn't you **(x)** *do the exam?*
B: I **(y)** *was too nervous to to through with it.*

(x) apply for the job
do the driving test
sing on TV
act in the play
fly the plane

(y) didn't have the courage to
just couldn't
couldn't
wasn't confident enough to
hadn't the courage to

TEST

A Fill in the spaces in this story:
June went . . . . dressmaking as a hobby, and her friends
persuaded her to go . . . . the local fashion competition.
She didn't want to because she thought she was too fat, but in the end
she went . . . . their suggestion. She went . . . . . . sweets
for a month to lose weight. June designed the dress herself, but her
mother went . . . . . . the design to check it.
  On the day of the competition June was too nervous to go . . . .
 . . . . . it and she stayed at home. Her friends were very dis-
because she went . . . . her promise.

B Replace the words in italics by a pronoun:
Example: He was too nervous to go through with *the exam.*
Answer: He was too nervous to go through with it.

1 I once went without *sleep* for three days.
2 Will you go over *these calculations* for me?

3 Your dog went for *my little girl* yesterday.
4 I don't go in for *tennis* but my brother does.
5 Don't go back on *that promise*, will you?

C Use one of the verbs you practised in this unit to make a remark that could follow each of these in a conversation:
Example: Did you really ask your boss for more money?
Possible Answers: I wanted to, but I couldn't go through with it.
                    I didn't have the courage to go through with it. etc.

1 What do you do for a hobby?
2 I'm getting rather fat. What should I do?
3 Why didn't Peter do the exam?
4 These new neighbours have a very fierce dog.
5 Poor Tom looked very pale when he came out of hospital.

Unit 3 – to put

She [3]put on the light.
She put the light on.
She put it on.

The story so far: Fred and Monica have just got engaged.

GUESTS FOR BREAKFAST

When George and his wife, Molly, heard that Fred and Monica were
engaged, they invited them for dinner one evening. They went there by
bus because Fred's car had broken down. They stayed late and missed
the last bus home, so George and Molly [3]put them up for the night.

5   The next morning they are all sitting at breakfast reading the
newspapers,

Molly: Oh dear! I see they're going to [3]put up the price of butter!
Fred: ([3]putting down his newspaper) And the train drivers are going
    on strike again.
10 George: Yes. They're [3]putting the clock back, if you ask me.
Monica: (crossly) I never understand half of what you say, George,
    What do you mean—'putting the clock back'?
George: (impatiently) You know! They're stopping progress. They're

going backwards instead of forwards.

15 **Monica:** I'll never understand politics. After we get married, I think I'll stop working and ³put my name down for some classes in politics. What do you think, Fred?

Fred: Well, er . . . you know, Monica . . .

George: (rudely) I wouldn't worry about it, Monica. SOME people
20 NEVER learn!

Monica: What!

(Silence. Monica is very angry. Molly gives George a pinch as she walks behind his chair to ³put on the light.)

Molly: Well, if you've all finished, I'll ³put away the things.
25 (Molly starts putting the breakfast things away. Monica gets up and ³puts on her coat, too angry to speak.)

Fred: Well, er . . . we'd better be going. Thanks very much for ³putting us up.

(Fred and Monica leave)

30 **George:** I can't stand that girl's stupidity. And Fred's going to bring her here again next week.

Molly: Don't worry. I'll ³put them off somehow.

At the bus stop:

Monica: I can't bear that man's rudeness! And you accepted their
35 invitation to go there again next week!

Fred: Don't worry. I'll ³put it off somehow.

QUESTIONS

Complete the answers. Use the words from the story.

1 Who had *given* Fred and Monica *a place to stay* for the night?
  George and Molly put them . . . . . . for the night. (line 4)
2 Are they going to *increase* or decrease the price of butter?
  They're going to put it . . . . . . (line 7)
3 Who thinks the train drivers are *stopping progress*?
  George thinks they're putting the clock . . . . . . (line 10)
4 What class does Monica think she should *enrol* for?
  She thinks she should put her name . . . . . . for a class in politics. (line 16)
5 Who said she would *put* the breakfast *things back in* the cupboard?
  Molly said she would put them . . . . . . (line 24)
6 Who said they would *postpone* the next visit?
  Molly and Fred both said they would put it . . . . . . (lines 32 and 36)
7 Did Fred pick up the newspaper?
  No. He put it . . . . . . (line 8)
8 Did Molly switch off the light?
  No. She put it . . . . . . (line 23)
9 Did Monica take off her coat?
  No. She put it . . . . . . (line 26)

EXERCISES

1 STRESS PRACTICE

Listen and repeat:

She put on the LIGHT.
She put the LIGHT on.
She put it ON.

He put down his PEN.
He put his PEN down.
He put it DOWN.

I'll put down my NAME.
I'll put my NAME down.
I'll put it DOWN.

He'll put off the NEXT VISIT.
He'll put the NEXT VISIT off.
He'll put it OFF.

This is the usual stress pattern, but it changes a lot with the meaning of the sentence:

Example: She didn't put the light ON. She switched it OFF.

2 PUT UP

Example: George and Molly *put* them *up* for the night.

George put up some friends for the night.
George put some friends up for the night.
George put them up for the night.

Make the same three sentences with each of these groups of words:

We . . . . . some relations . . . . . . for a few days.
I . . . . . Tom . . . . . . till he found a flat.
Can you . . . . . . my cousin . . . . . for tonight?

3 PUT DOWN

PUT ON

Example: Fred *put down* his newspaper.
Molly *put* the light *on*.
Monica *put* her coat *on*.

Cue: Take you gloves off.   *Response:* But I've just put them on!
Pick up that bag.   But I've just put it down!
Switch the radio off.   But I've just put it on!

Now give the response to the following cues.

Take your coat off.
Pick up these suitcases.
Take you hat off.
Put the lights off.

Pick up that box.
Switch the TV off.
Pick you bag up.
Pick up the baby.

Note: For things that burn, we *light* them, and then *put* them *out*. We also say, 'Put out the light'.

4 PUT DOWN

Example: 'I'll *put* my name *down* for some classes in politics,' said Monica.

Cue: an art class . . . . . . a music class

Response   Student A: Did you put your name down for *an art class*?
             Student B: No. I put it down for *a music class*.

Now give the responses to the following cues.

Mr Smith's class . . . . . . Mr Brown's class
an elementary class . . . . . . an advanced class
a morning class . . . . . . an evening class
a French course . . . . . . an English course
some driving lessons . . . . . . some skiing instruction
the bus trip to Oxford . . . . . . the trip to Brighton

5 PUT UP

Example: 'They're going to *put up* the price of butter,' said Molly.

DIALOGUE PRACTICE:

A: Who puts up (**x**) *the price of meat?*

B: I think the butchers put it up.

OR

I don't know who puts it up. It just goes up.

(**x**) **Substitute:** The price of bread / the price of milk / our fees / the cost of transport / the price of cigarettes / the taxes / workers' wages / the price of eggs

6 PUT AWAY

Example: Molly starts *putting away* the breakfast things.

Cue: bread . . . . . . cupboard

Response: Student A: Shall I put the *bread* in the *cupboard* now?
             Student B: Yes. Put it away.

Now give the responses to the following cues.

knives . . . . . . drawer	tablecloth . . . . . . cupboard
biscuits . . . . . . box	shirts . . . . . . wardrobe
milk . . . . . . fridge	books . . . . . . my bag

7 PUT OFF

Example: 'I'll *put* them *off* somehow,' said Molly.
           'I'll *put* it *off* somehow,' said Fred.

i. If you don't want to see a person you can put them off by, for example, saying you are ill. Discuss ways in which a secretary puts people off when her boss doesn't want to see them or speak to them on the phone. *Example:* She puts them off by saying . . . . .

ii. You put off something till later. *Example:* going to the dentist, a visit, a wedding, a meeting, a discussion, a holiday, doing your homework, etc. **Write about two of these:**
I put off . . . . . . because . . . . . .
I put . . . . . . off because . . . . . .

TEST

A Fill in the spaces in this story:

I had put my name . . . . . . for an evening class and was getting ready to go to the first lesson. I had just put . . . . . . my coat, and was putting . . . . . . the lights when the doorbell rang. It was a very rude young man who put . . . . . . his suitcase, introduced himself as a friend of my nephew, and asked if I could put him . . . . . . for the night. I tried to put him . . . . . . but he was determined to stay. I had to put . . . . . . going to my class and *put up with his company for the whole evening.

* *Note:* to ²put up with - meaning to bear e.g. I can't put up with that man's rudeness.

B Replace the words in italics by a pronoun.
Example: I'll put on *my hat.*
Answer: I'll put it on.

1 He put down *his heavy suitcases.*
2 We can't possibly put *your friend* up tonight.
3 She put down *her name* for some tennis coaching.
4 They put up *the price of eggs* only last week.
5 You can put away *your books* now.

C. Use one of the verbs you practised in this unit to make a remark that could follow each of these in a conversation:
Example: Are you going to go to any evening classes this term?
Possible Answers: Yes. I've put my name down for a history class.
I'm putting my name down for a course in politics, etc.

1 It's getting very cold and dark in this room.
2 This suitcase is terribly heavy.
3 You're too busy to keep your appointment at the dentist's tomorrow.
4 My cousin will be visiting your town next week and all the hotels are full. Can you help him?
5 It's Mr Smith again, sir. He wants to speak to you on the phone. Will you take the call this time?

Unit 4 – to make

Monica was ³making up her face.
Monica was making her face up.
Monica was making it up.

They were ²making for the vicarage.
They were making for it.

The story so far: Fred is engaged to Monica, but he doesn't want to get married.

ON THE WAY TO THE *VICARAGE

Fred didn't take Monica with him when he bought the engagement ring, and he bought a secondhand one because it was cheaper. It was a nice one, but Monica was very angry that it wasn't new. They quarrelled about it and shouted at each other for hours, but in the end they
5 ³made it up. Fred felt very guilty about buying a cheap ring, so to ²make up for it he promised that they would go to the vicarage the next day to make the arrangements for the wedding.
   So at three o'clock the next afternoon Fred and Monica were ²making for the vicarage in Fred's newly repaired car. When Monica
10 had finished ³making up her face, she took a piece of paper from her bag and frowned at what was written on it.
   'Molly's writing is terrible!' she said crossly. 'She wrote down the vicar's address for me but I can't ³make it out at all. I know it's in Green Street, but it's impossible to make out the number.'

30

15 'Then we'd better go home,' said Fred at once, and he turned the car round.

Monica started to cry. For a moment Fred just sat there with his head in his hands. Then he quickly ³made up his mind. Before Monica could stop crying and start shouting, he turned the car round again and **20** drove on.

On the corner of Green Street were two men looking at the engine of their old car. One of them was on crutches. Fred parked his car in front of them. Before he could ask for directions, one of the men said, 'Thank you for stopping, sir. Could you and your wife please push my **25** car? It won't start. And my friend can't help me. He's *lame.'

So Fred and Monica got behind the car and pushed it. They were surprised that it started so quickly, and that at the same time they heard another car starting and driving off . . .

It was Fred's car! The man had ³made up the story in order to trick **30** them, and the 'lame' man had ²made off with Fred's car.

* 'The Vicarage' is the vicar's house. A vicar is a Church of England priest.

* lame: unable to walk.

QUESTIONS

Complete the answers. Use the words from the story.
1 Did Fred and Monica *make friends again after their quarrel*?
  Yes. They made it . . . . . . in the end. (line 5)
2 Fred *felt sorry* because he had bought a cheap ring. What did he *do to compensate* for it?
  To make . . . . it he promised to take her to the vicarage the next day. (line 6)
3 At three o'clock were they *going in the direction of* the vicarage?
  Yes. They were making . . . . . . the vicarage. (line 9)
4 Was Monica *putting on make-up* in the car?
  Yes. She was making . . . . . . her face. (line 10)
5 Why couldn't Monica *read* what was written on the piece of paper?
  She couldn't make it . . . . . . because of the bad writing. (line 13)
6 When Monica started to cry, what did Fred *decide* to do?
  He made . . . . . . his mind to go to the vicarage. (line 18)
7 Did the man *invent* the story about his lame friend, or was it the truth?
  It wasn't the truth. He made it . . . . . . (line 29)
8 Who *stole and escaped with* Fred's car?
  The 'lame' man made . . . . it. (line 30)

EXERCISES

1 STRESS PRACTICE

Listen and repeat:
The dog WENT for MONICA.
The dog WENT for her.
They were MAKING for the VICARAGE.
They were MAKING for it.

2 MAKE FOR

Example: Fred and Monica were *making for* the vicarage.

Cue: the town
Response: I was making for *the town* when my car broke down.

Now give the responses to the following cues.
the beach / the city / when I met my friend / when I had an accident /
when I saw Mary / the door / the telephone / when it stopped ringing

3 STRESS PRACTICE

Listen and repeat:

George went IN for HUNTING.
George went IN for it.
Don't go BACK on your PROMISE.
Don't go BACK on it.
Fred made UP for BUYING it.
Fred made UP for it.
The lame man made OFF with FRED'S CAR.
The lame man made OFF with it.

4 MAKE UP FOR

Example: Fred felt sorry about buying a cheap ring. To *make up for* it he promised to go to the vicarage.

Cue: Fred felt guilty about it, but he *promised to go to the vicarage*, didn't he?
Response: Yes. He made up for it by promising to go to the vicarage.

Now give the responses to the following cues.
Mary was rude to her friend, but she *apologized*, didn't she?
You were impolite to your friend, but you *apologized*, didn't you?
You lost your brother's book, but you *bought him a new one*, didn't you?
You smoked all your friend's cigarettes, but you *bought him a packet of cigarettes later*, didn't you?
The waiter spilt some soup on your clothes, but he *paid for the*

dry cleaning, didn't he?

Tom was very lazy in class, but he *brought the teacher some flowers,* didn't he?

5 MAKE OFF WITH

Example: The 'lame' man *made off with* Fred's car.

Cue: bag

Response *Student A:* My bag has gone.

Student B: Perhaps somebody's made off with it.

Now give the responses to the following cues.

purse / money / books / suitcases / bicycle / watch

6 STRESS PRACTICE

Listen and repeat:

They made up the QUARREL.   He made up his MIND.
They made the QUARREL up.   He made his MIND up.
They made it UP.   He made it UP.

7 MAKE OUT

Example: 'Molly wrote down the address, but I can't *make* it *out,*' said Monica.

With Pattern 3 Verbs we can say: I can't make out *the address.*
                                   I can't make *the address* out.
                                   I can't make *it* out.

The object of the verb is 'the address', and this is very short.

Now look at the same sentence with a long object:

I can't make *what she has written on the paper* out.

Here the two parts of the verb are too far apart.

With a long object it is better to say:

I can't make out *what she has written on the paper.*

Use the best pattern for these. Begin, 'I can't make . . .':

what he's saying to me	the words of the song he's singing
the words	the number
them	his writing
the name of the street	the instructions for this exercise
it	what the teacher is saying

8 MAKE UP
Example: Monica finished *making up* her face.

DIALOGUE PRACTICE:
Mother: You shouldn't make up your face in the bus.
Girl: And why shouldn't I make it up there?
Mother: You should make your face up before you leave home, and
not outside!
**Now make up a conversation between the same girl and her boss
when she starts to make up her face in the office.**

9 MAKE UP
Example: Fred *made up* his mind.

**Choose the right ending for the sentences in A from the section
marked B.**
A. They took a long time . . . . . .
   She very quickly . . . . . .
   Will he ever . . . . . .
   I can't . . . . . .
   Haven't you . . . . . .
   We shouldn't . . . . . .

B. made up her mind to buy it.
   make up his mind?
   make up my mind about it.
   made it up yet?
   make our minds up too quickly.
   to make up their minds about it.

10 MAKE UP
Example: The man had *made up* the story in order to trick them.

DIALOGUE PRACTICE:
Teacher: Did you make up (x) *that song* yourself or did somebody else
make it up?
Boy: Of course not! I made *that song* up all by myself!

(x) **Substitute:** that composition / these poems / that story / that play /
these jokes / that lie

TEST

A Fill in the spaces in this story:
'Somebody's made . . . . my pen!' someone shouted loudly
from the back of the classroom. Mr Ships turned round quickly and
tried to make . . . . . . who had shouted. The class was silent. Mr Ships
made . . . . . . his mind to find out who it was. He was making . . . . . .

34

the back of the classroom when he saw Susie Brown making . . . . . .
her face under the desk. Mr Ships was very angry with Susan, and at
the end of the lesson she cleaned the blackboard to make . . . . . .
. . . . . . it. But Mr Ships never found out who had shouted.

B Replace the words in italics by a pronoun:

Example: I don't want to make up *my face* today.
Answer: I don't want to make it up.

1 Somebody's made off with *my money*.
2 How can I make up for *what I've done*?
3 Don't believe her stories - she's always making up *lies*.
4 I can't make out *what he's saying*.
5 My girlfriend doesn't want to make up *the quarrel*.

C Replace the words in italics by the words in brackets. Give *two* answers wherever you can:

Example: I can't make *it* out. (what she's written on the paper)
Answer: I can't make out what she's written on the paper.
      (only one answer here)

1 I couldn't make *it* out. (what you were saying on the phone)
2 He's always making *them* up. (silly stories)
3 Did he make *it* up? (the story he told us yesterday)
4 He switched *them* off. (the lights in the hall, the heater and the TV)
5 I put *it* on. (my coat)

Unit 5 – to come

George ²came across a book.
George came across it.

The book had just ¹come out.

The story so far: Fred's car has just been stolen.

GEORGE GOES MOUNTAINEERING

George ²came across an interesting book about mountaineering. It had just ¹come out. It was written by a man who ²came into a fortune, then stopped work and spent the rest of his life climbing mountains. When he had finished reading it, George phoned Fred.

5 **George:** I say, Fred, why don't we go mountaineering?
Fred: No thanks, George. I've just lost my car. Somebody stole it.
George: Oh, I say, what bad luck! When did it happen?
Fred: Just now. This afternoon.
George: Well, don't worry about it. Why don't you ¹come round for a
10 drink?
Fred: I'd really rather not just now, George.
George: Oh, ¹come on! I want to show you this book about

36

mountaineering. Just ¹come over for a few minutes and I'll show it to you.

15 Fred: Oh, well, all right then. But I'm not climbing any mountains!

Twenty minutes later Fred knocked on the door of George's house. His wife, Molly, opened the door.

''Come in,' said Molly. 'George is in his study.'

When Fred went into the study, George was sitting on top of a ladder **20** reading his book.

''Come on up,' he said. 'It gives you the feeling of being a mountaineer.'

'No. You ¹come down and we'll talk about it,' said Fred rather impatiently, and when George didn't reply, 'Now do ¹come along! I **25** haven't got all day, and I think you're being silly about this mountaineering.'

George was very annoyed at this, so he turned round quickly to say something to Fred. The ladder overbalanced, and he started to fall. He grabbed at the light cord, but it ¹came away in his hand. George **30** crashed heavily on to the floor and was completely unconscious for a few minutes. When he ¹came to, Molly was fanning him with the mountaineering book.

'I hope YOU never come into a fortune!' she said.

QUESTIONS

Complete the answers. Use the words from the story.

1 Who was *not looking for it but just happened to find* a book about mountaineering?
George came . . . . . . it. (line 1)
2 Had the book been *published* a long time ago?
No. It had just come . . . . . . (line 2)
3 Who *inherited* a fortune?
The author of the book came . . . . . . a fortune. (line 2)
4 Who invited Fred *to come and visit* him?
George invited Fred to come over. 'Come . . . . . . for a drink,' he said. (line 9)
5 When Fred said he didn't want to come round for a drink, what did George say *to persuade* him?
He said, 'Come . . . . . . !' and he told him about the book. (line 12)
6 When George wouldn't come ⌄down from the ladder, Fred *got impatient and told him to hurry up*, didn't he?
Yes. He said, 'Now do come . . . . . . ! I haven't got all day.' (line 24)
7 What *broke off in* George's *hand* when he was trying to save himself?
The light cord came . . . . . . in his hand. (line 29)
8 When did George *become conscious again*?
He came . . . . . after a few minutes. (line 31)

EXERCISES

1 STRESS PRACTICE

Listen and repeat:

That dog will GO for MONICA.
They were MAKING for the VICARAGE.
George CAME across a BOOK.
He CAME into a FORTUNE.

2 COME ACROSS

Example: George *came across* an interesting book.

Cue: this book
Response: I came across *this book* just by chance.

Now give the responses to the following cues.
this old vase / these letters / just by accident / in a second hand shop
this restaurant / this job / that picture / in the study / recently / in an
advertisement

3 COME INTO

Example: The author *came into* a fortune, then stopped work and
spent the rest of his life climbing mountains.

Imagine that you have a very rich uncle and that when he dies you
may come into some money or some property. **Write a sentence
about this.**

4 STRESS PRACTICE

Listen and repeat:

Come UP.
No, you come DOWN.
Come ROUND for a drink.
It came AWAY in his hand.
When he came TO she was fanning him with a book.

5 COME OVER/COME ROUND

Example: '*Come over* for a few minutes.'
'*Come round* for a drink.'

Cue: for a meal
Response: When can you come round *for a meal?*

Now give the responses to the following cues.
for dinner / to my place / come over / for a drink / come round / I / to
your place / to see you

6 COME OUT

Example: The book had just *come out.*

Cue: How often is 'The Times' published? Every day?
Response: Yes. It comes out every day.

Now give the responses to the following cues.

How often is 'The Guardian' published? Every day?
How often is the 'Evening News' published? Every evening?
How often is the 'Woman's Weekly' published? Once a week?
When was that book published? Some time ago?
When was that film first shown? Last year?

Make up sentences about other newspapers, magazines, books or films that you know.

7 COME ON/COME ALONG

Example: 'Oh, *come on.* I want to show you this book,' said George.
'Now do *come along*! I haven't got all day!' said Fred.

DIALOGUE PRACTICE:

A: I'll never learn to change gears.
 drive.
 turn corners.

B: Now come on. You're doing very well.

A: Thanks. It's really nice of you to be so encouraging. But why
is that policeman shouting at us?
 waving

B: Come on! He wants us to move faster. Oh, come along! You're
holding up the traffic!

A: Well, don't get so angry. I'm only a learner.
 impatient. beginner.
 cross.

Notice that 'Come on!' can be encouraging or impatient, depending on how it is said, but 'Come along! usually suggests impatience.

8 COME AWAY

Example: He grabbed at the light cord, but it *came away* in his hand.

Imagine that you visited a very old house. **Make up sentences from this table to describe what happened:**

The door knob		in my hand.
The knocker		when I tried it.
The bell rope		when I pulled it.
The curtain	came away	when I touched it.
The window		as soon as I touched it.
The tap		
The cupboard door		

Now imagine that you tried to drive a very old car. **Write three sentences about what happened.** Use these words: the steering wheel; the gear lever; the hand brake.

9 COME TO/COME ROUND
Example: When he *came to*, Molly was fanning him with a book.

DIALOGUE PRACTICE:
Practice reading this dialogue in a group of five people:

A: What's happened?
B: This man's unconscious, but I think he'll *come round* in a few minutes.
A: Well, you should do something to *bring* him *round*.
C: Yes, *bring* him *round* by fanning him.
D: *Bring* him *round* by slapping his face.
Man: Ohhhhhhhhhhh!
B: Shh! He's *coming round* anyway.
Man: Ohhhhh! My head!
A: Now lie down! You've been unconscious and you've just *come round*.
Man: Ohhh! My head! What happened?

Now read the dialogue again using *come to*
bring him round

TEST

A Fill in the spaces in this story:
The late edition of the 'Evening News' always comes . . . . . . at about five o'clock. I had bought a copy and was reading it on my way home when I suddenly came . . . . . . an announcement that Sir Gayelord Greenleaf had died. My mind went completely blank with surprise and shock for a very long time. When I came . . . . . . I realized that the bus had gone a long way past my stop.

I jumped up and must have pulled the bell cord much too hard for it came . . . . . . in my hand. The bus conductor was very angry.

'Come . . . . . . , sir!' he said impatiently as I walked slowly in a dream to the back of the bus.

I had walked half a mile when I came . . . . . . a telephone box. With shaking hands, I dialled my brother's telephone number.

'Come . . . . . . for a drink. We should celebrate!' he said excitedly. I couldn't reply. 'Marvellous news!' he went on. 'We should both come . . . . . . a lot of money!'

I hung up.

B Complete this dialogue using the verbs in brackets:

1 He: . . . . ? (come round/over)
   She: No thanks. I must be getting home.
2 He: . . . . ! Here's my car. (come on)
   She: Ooh! Isn't it super! Where did you find it? In an advertisement?
3 He: . . . . (come across)
   She: It's the very latest model, isn't it?
4 He: . . . . (come out)
   She: How could you afford to buy it?
5 He: . . . . (come into)
   She: Really? Well, in that case I'll accept your invitation for a drink!

C Use one of the verbs you practised in this unit to make a remark that could follow each of these in a conversation:

Example: I don't want to swim. The water's too cold.
Possible answers: Oh, come on!
                    Come on! The water's lovely.
                                              etc.

1 This is a new book, isn't it?
2 How did you break the handle of that teacup?
3 Will he stay unconscious for very long, doctor?
4 What a beautiful old vase! Where did you find it?
5 Her grandfather is very rich and she's the only child, isn't she?

Unit 6 – to call

A doctor must be ³called IN.
His prescription must be ²CALLED for.

The story so far: Fred doesn't want to get married, but he is engaged to Monica. On their way to the vicarage to arrange the wedding, Fred's car is stolen. Fred promises to take her to the vicarage by taxi the next day.

A FRIEND IN NEED - PART I

Fred was eating his breakfast and feeling very unhappy when the telephone rang. It was George's wife, Molly.

Molly: I'm sorry, Fred. I know I shouldn't phone you up so early.
Fred: That's all right. How are you? How is George?
5 **Molly:** He's not well. We had to ³call a doctor in last night.
Fred: Poor George! Can I do anything to help?
Molly: Yes, Fred. Are you doing anything this morning?
Fred: Well, I had arranged something, but it's not important. I'll ³call it off and come and see George, of course.
10 **Molly:** And could you ²call for his prescription at the chemist's shop? It should be ready now.
Fred: Of course.

Molly: Thanks very much, Fred. I'm so glad we can ²call on a friend like you when we need help.

15 **Fred:** Oh, it's nothing, Molly. I'm still having breakfast, so you can ³call me back if you think of anything else you want. I'm really very happy to help you.

QUESTIONS

Complete the answers. Use the words from the story.

1 Why did Molly *ask a doctor to come and treat* George?
She called a doctor . . . . . . because he was ill. (line 5)

2 Why did Fred say he would *cancel* the arrangement he had made with Monica?
He said he would call it . . . . . . and visit George. (line 9)

3 What did Molly ask Fred *to go and collect from* the chemist's shop?
She asked him to call . . . . . . George's prescription. (line 10)

4 Who can Molly *ask to help her* when she needs help?
She can call . . . . . . Fred. (line 13)

5 Why did Fred tell Molly she could *phone* him *again*?
He said she could call him . . . . . . if she wanted anything else. (line 16)

A FRIEND IN NEED - PART II

Fred felt very happy. He had a marvellous excuse now and could call off his arrangement with Monica. He quickly dialled Monica's number:

'Er . . . hello . . . Is that you, Mrs Brown? Isn't Monica up yet? . . . No! Please don't bother to call her. Could you give her a message? Could you tell her that our arrangement for today must be ³called OFF . . . . . . Well, as you know, Mrs Brown . . . er . . . I can always be ²CALLED on to help when help is needed, and . . . er, today I must help someone who is seriously ill. His prescription must be ²CALLED for, and . . . er . . . a specialist must be ³called IN. I must leave here immediately. Goodbye.'

Fred hung up quickly. 'It's marvellous,' he thought, 'how something always seems to happen to save me from marrying Monica. I wonder what will happen next time. I only hope I won't be ³called UP by the army!'

Note: During this phone conversation Fred spoke in a special way for two reasons:

1 He didn't want Monica's mother to know who he was helping. So instead of saying, 'Molly can always call on me to help,' he said, 'I can always be called on to help.'

2 He was trying to sound very formal and important. He could have said, 'I must call for his prescription.' But it sounded more important when he said, 'His prescription must be called for.'

This is the *Passive*. Not all Pattern 2 and 3 Verbs can be made passive. At the beginning of each exercise an example will be given if the verb can be made passive. Pattern 1 Verbs cannot be made passive, as they have no object.

EXERCISES

1 STRESS PRACTICE

Listen and repeat:
Fred can be CALLED on.
His prescription must be CALLED for.

2 CALL ON
Example: Molly can *call on* Fred when she needs help.
Passive:　Fred can be CALLED on when she needs help.

i. **Make sentences from this table:**

They	could			a friend	to help.
We	can			Fred	in an emergency.
Mary	will	call on		the neighbours	if something happens.
I	might			you	if something goes wrong.
Tom	should			them	if help is needed.
She	must			my mother	

Example: They must call on the neighbours if something goes wrong.

ii. **Now make passive sentences:**

A friend	could			to help.
Fred	can			in an emergency.
The neighbours	will	be called on		if something happens.
You	might			if something goes wrong.
They	should			if help is needed.
My mother	must			

Example: The neighbours must be called on if something goes wrong.

44

3 CALL FOR
Example: Fred must *call for* the prescription.
Passive: The prescription must be CALLED for.

DIALOGUE PRACTICE
A: (x) *These parcels* must be called for.
B: Who should call for them?
A: Mr Smith must call for them.
B: And when could they be called for?
after six.

A: They can be called for any time.
tomorrow.

(x) **Substitute:** these clothes / this cheque / these letters / the money.

4 STRESS PRACTICE
Listen and repeat
Fred might be called UP.
A doctor should be called IN.
The arrangement must be called OFF.

5 CALL OFF
Example: I must *call off* the arrangement.
Passive: The arrangement must be called OFF.

Cue: It's going to rain. They *might* call the tennis match off.
Response: That's right. It *might* be called off.

Now give the responses to the following cues.
It's going to rain. They *might* call the cricket match off.
Her mother has just died. She *must* call the party off.
The conductor is ill. I think they *will* call off the concert.
His father is very ill. He *should* call off his trip abroad.
We haven't got everybody's phone number. So we *can't* call the meeting off.
We knew it was going to rain. But we *couldn't* call the garden party off.

6 CALL IN
Example: I must *call in* a specialist.
Passive: A specialist must be called IN.

DIALOGUE PRACTICE
A Should we call a (x) *doctor in?*

B Yes. One must be called in at once.
immediately.

(x) **Substitute:** specialist / expert / electrician / plumber.

7 CALL UP

Example: 'I hope I won't be called UP by the army,' thought Fred.
This expression is nearly always passive.

Practice these questions. Give your opinion in the answers:

QUESTIONS			ANSWERS
Will	young men		Yes, of course.
Can	young women		I think so.
Could	old people	be called up in a war?	Perhaps.
Might	children		I don't think so.
Should	you		I'm not sure.
	your father		Definitely not.
			etc.

8 CALL BACK

Example: 'You can *call* me *back*,' Fred said to Molly.

DIALOGUE PRACTICE

Boss: Ring / Phone **(x)** *Mr Brown* for me, please.

Secretary: Hello. Could I speak to Mr Brown, please?

Voice: I'm afraid he's busy / out at the moment. Could you call him / he call you back?

(x) Substitute: Mr Smith / Miss Jones / the Director / Mrs Robinson.

TEST

**A Which one of the words in capital letters should be stressed?
Underline it.**

Example: He's ill. A doctor must be CALLED IN.
Answer: · He's ill. A doctor must be CALLED IN.

1 It's raining. The match will probably be CALLED OFF.
2 This parcel must be CALLED FOR.
3 I think an expert should be CALLED IN.
4 Mary can't be CALLED ON in an emergency.
5 In some countries young men must be CALLED UP for two years.

B Write these sentences again in the passive:
Example: You must call off your holiday.
Answer: Your holiday must be called off.

1 They might call him up to do national service.

2 Somebody should call for it after three o'clock.
3 Don't worry! I'll call a doctor in.
4 Will you call in a specialist too?
5 I couldn't call the meeting off.
6 Mrs Robinson can call on Tom when she needs help. (Use 'by Mrs Robinson' in your answer.)

C **Use one of the verbs you practised in this unit to make a remark that could follow each of these in a conversation. Make it passive whenever you can:**

Example: This horse is very ill.
*Possible Answers:*Yes. We must call in a vet at once.
A vet must be called in immediately.

1 This child is very ill.
2 When will Tom do his national service?
3 I haven't time to go to the dry cleaners to collect these clothes. Could you get them on your way home?
4 Do you think you can ask your little sister to help if something goes wrong?
5 Hello . . . . . yes . . . . . I'm sorry, the manager is out at the moment.

Review – Units 1-6

Unit 1
1 What went OFF at eight o'clock?
2 Whose work wasn't going AHEAD?
3 Who said he was going AWAY?

Unit 2
4 Who did George's dog GO for?
5 What did Fred go WITHOUT?
6 Which plan was he going OVER?
7 What hobby did George go IN for?
8 Which promise couldn't Fred go BACK on?

Unit 3
9 Who did George and Molly put UP?
10 What did Molly put ON?
11 What did Monica put ON?
12 What will Fred and Molly both put OFF?
13 Who couldn't George put UP with?

Unit 4
14 Where were they MAKING for when Fred's car was stolen?
15 What couldn't Monica make OUT?
16 What story did the thieves make UP?
17 What did the thieves make OFF with?

Unit 5
18 What did George come ACROSS?
19 When had the book come OUT?
20 What came AWAY in George's hand?
21 When did George come TO?

Unit 6
22 Who had Molly called IN?
23 Who was CALLED on to help?
24 Who might be called UP?

Unit 7 – to run

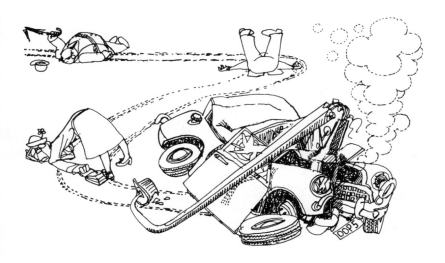

The thieves [3]ran three people down.
Three people were run DOWN.
The car [2]ran into a lamp-post.
This lamp-post was RUN into by a car.

The Story so far: Fred doesn't want to get married, but he is engaged to Monica. His car has been stolen.

UNEXPECTED NEWS

After work Fred went to a pub. As usual, his money had [1]run out before pay day. But he was [3]running up a few bills because he hoped it wouldn't be long before he might get the insurance money for his stolen car. He had given up hope of the police ever finding it. So Fred sat
5 drinking a beer and trying to listen to his transistor radio. It didn't work well enough because the batteries were [3]run down. He was looking through the local newspaper instead when an interesting headline caught his eye:

Snake Escapes – Car Thieves Caught

10　For some time now police have been trying to catch a gang of car thieves in the Folkestone area. Early this morning they surrounded the gang in a house in Slumton. When two of the men ¹ran away the police ²ran after them, and they made off in one of their stolen cars. The police pursued them, and during the chase three pedestrians were

15　³run down. The thieves did not stop till the car swerved to avoid ²running over a snake. The driver lost control, and the car ²ran into a lamp-post. The stolen car was completely smashed up. It is said to have belonged to a Mr Frederick Smith, whom the police are trying to contact.

20　'That's my car! shouted Fred. He jumped up and was making for the telephone when he ²ran into George.

'Hello, Fred! Fancy seeing you here! Have you seen the news?'

'Yes. Just now.'

'Well, you'll get your insurance money now. What are you going to

25　do?'

'I'm going to phone up my boss and ask for some time off.'

'Why?'

'I think I need a holiday and now I can afford one.'

'Yes. You have been looking a bit ³run down. Where will you go?'

30　'I think I'll go to Brighton,' whispered Fred. 'But don't tell Monica, will you?'

QUESTIONS

Complete the answers. Use the words from the story.

1　Fred's money was *finished*, wasn't it?
　Yes. His money had ¹run . . . . . . (line 1)

2　Who was *buying things and promising to pay later?*
　Fred was running . . . . . . bills. (line 2)

3　Fred's radio didn't work very well. Were the batteries *weak*?
　Yes. The batteries were run . . . . . . (line 6)

4　How many of the thieves *escaped* when the police arrived?
　Two of them ran . . . . . (line 12)

5　What did they do when the police *chased* them?
　When the police ran . . . . . . them they made off in one of their stolen cars. (line 13)

6　How many pedestrians *were hit and knocked down by the car*?
　Three pedestrians were run . . . . . . (line 15)

7　Why didn't the thief *drive over the top of* the snake?
　He didn't want to run . . . . . . it because he was afraid of snakes. (line 16)

8　The car *stopped because it hit* a lamp-post, didn't it?
　Yes. It ran . . . . . . a lamp-post. (line 16)

50

9 Fred *hadn't arranged to meet* George, *but he just happened to see him by chance*, didn't he?
   Yes. He ran . . . . . . George just by chance. (line 21)
10 Why did Fred need a holiday? Was he *feeling tired and weak*?
   Perhaps he was run . . . . , but probably he really just wanted to run . . . . Monica! (line 29)

EXERCISES

1 STRESS PRACTICE

Listen and repeat:
The car RAN into a LAMP POST.
Fred RAN into GEORGE in the pub.
The lamp post was RUN into by a car.

2 RUN OVER
  RUN INTO
  Example: The car swerved to avoid *running over* a snake, and it *ran into* a lamp post.
  Passive: This lamp post was RUN into by a car.
  This expression is less often passive.

i.
Cue: What happened to that lamp post?
                   bus
Response: A   car ran into it.
                   lorry

                              bus.
              OR It was run into by a   car.
                              lorry.

Now give the responses to the following cues.
What happened to your wall?
How did your car get smashed up?
What happened to these sign posts?
How did that tree fall down?
How did these bicycles get damaged?
How did that shop window get smashed up?

ii.
Cue: a tree   *Response:* My car ran into *a tree.*
          a stick   My car ran over *a stick.*

Now give the responses to the following cues.
a lamp post / a brick / some nails / a bus / some stones / a piece of glass / an elephant / a mouse

3 RUN INTO

Example: Fred was making for the telephone when he *ran into* George.

Cue: in the post office
Response: I'm always running into people *in the post-office.*

Now give the responses to the following cues.

in town / when I'm shopping / when I'm on holiday / in the street / when I don't want to / my boss / my friends / Bill / people / my neighbour

4 STRESS PRACTICE

Listen and repeat:
The men ran AWAY.
They ran AWAY from the POLICE.
His money had run OUT.
He had run OUT of MONEY.

5 RUN AWAY
RUN AFTER

Example: Two of the men *ran away.*
The police *ran after* them.

Cue: a policeman . . . . . the men
Response: A *policeman* ran after *the men*, but they ran away from him.

Now give the responses to the following cues.

a policeman . . . . . the children	the bull . . . . . me
some policemen . . . . . . the thieves	I . . . . . the thief
a dog . . . . . . the children	the policeman . . . . . . me
the children . . . . . . a cat	Monica . . . . . . Fred

6 RUN OUT

Example: Fred's money had *run out* before pay day.

Cue: petrol.
Response: Student A: The *petrol* has nearly run out.

       Student B: You ran out of $\begin{smallmatrix} \text{petrol} \\ \text{it} \end{smallmatrix}$ yesterday too!

Now give the responses to the following cues.
water/paper/bread/gas/money/time/my patience/my ideas

7 STRESS PRACTICE

Listen and repeat:
He ran up a few BILLS.
He ran a few BILLS up.

He ran them UP.
The batteries were run DOWN.
Three people were run DOWN.
You're looking a bit run DOWN.

8 RUN UP

Example: He *ran up* a few bills.

Use this expression in sentences beginning:

You mustn't . . . . . .   I know I oughtn't to . . . . . .
He shouldn't . . . . . .   I'm always telling him not to . . . . .
Fred is always . . . . . .   It's silly to . . . . . .

9 RUN DOWN

Example: The batteries were *run DOWN*

This expression is nearly always passive.

Make questions about these sentences beginning 'why':

The batteries are run down.   Why . . . . . . ?
She's always run down.   Why . . . . . . ?
I'm feeling run down.   Why . . . . . . ?
He looks rather run down.   Why . . . . . . ?
The battery's run down.   Why . . . . . . ?

10 RUN DOWN

Example: The thieves *ran* three people *down*.
Passive: Three people were ru.. DOWN.

DIALOGUE PRACTICE:

Practise reading this dialogue in a group of five people.

Thief: Stop the car. You ran somebody *down*. An old lady, I think.

Driver: I didn't run the old lady *down*. It was the police car that ran her *down*. Anyway, I'm not stopping.

(Later, at the hospital.)

Nurse: How was this old lady run *down*?

Ambulance
Man: The police were chasing some thieves, and I think she was run *down* by the police car.

Old Lady: No, I wasn't. I was run *down* by these car thieves. You'll read about it in the newspapers tomorrow!

Now read the dialogue again using: run over. When used as a *Pattern 3 Verb*, this has the same meaning as 'run down'.

TEST

A Fill in the spaces in this story:
I ran . . . . . . my old friend Susan the other day and we talked about
old times, especially about the day she took her driving test. Susan
couldn't afford to run a car, but she had bought one, so she was always
running . . . . money. When the petrol ran . . . . . . she
would get petrol on credit. She ran . . . . . . bills at several garages.
She was always leaving the lights on, so the batteries were usually
run . . . . . .
Susan ran into trouble when she went to take her driving test.
Outside the police station she nearly ran a policeman . . . . . . The car
swerved and she ran . . . . . . the back of a bus. She got out of the car
and ran . . . . . . The policeman ran . . . . . . her. Susan never drove a
car again.

B Write these sentences again in the passive:
Example: The thieves ran me over.
Answer: I was run over by the thieves.

1 A bus ran the little girl down.
2 A lorry ran into the back of my car.
3 A bull ran after us.
4 If you leave the lights on you'll run the batteries down.
5 Every day careless drivers run people over.

**C Use one of the verbs you practised in this unit to make a remark that
could follow each of these in a conversation:**
Example: Shall I go shopping and pay later? I haven't any money.
Possible Answers: It's silly to run up bills etc.

1 Why won't your car start? Is there something wrong with the
batteries?
2 I haven't seen Tom for ages. You said you met him the other day.
Where was it?
3 Why didn't you finish painting the house? Didn't you have enough
paint?
4 Good heavens! What happened to the back of your car?
5 Good heavens! What happened to the front of your car?

Unit 8 – to turn

So many girls have ³turned me down.
I've been turned DOWN by so many girls.

The story so far: Fred and Monica are engaged, but Fred doesn't want
to get married. His car has been stolen, and when he gets his insurance
money he decides to escape to Brighton for a holiday.

FRED IN BRIGHTON

Fred felt more relaxed than he had for years. He had spent his first day
in Brighton lying on the beach sunbathing. Now he stood at the window
of his hotel room watching the girls go by. Suddenly he caught sight of
two girls who were sitting outside the café just across the road. One of
5 them was very pretty.

   'Hm! That one really *³turns me on!' thought Fred enthusiastically.
'I wonder if I could ask her out to the cinema. She'd probably ³turn me
down, I suppose. I've been turned down by so many girls,' he thought
sadly. But he ³turned the idea over a few times and decided to try.
10 Quickly combing his hair, he left the room, forgetting to ³turn the radio
off or lock the door.

   Fred ³turned on the charm and offered to buy the girls a drink.

They were very friendly, and introduced themselves. The pretty one's
name was Jeanette and her friend was called Susan. Susan was clever,
15 and she could see that Fred really fancied her friend. So when Fred
suggested that they all go to the cinema, Susan ²turned to Jeanette
and said, 'You go, Jeanette. I'm going to ¹turn in early tonight. I'm
very tired.' So Jeanette and Fred arranged to meet at eight o'clock, and
Fred was sure he had never felt so happy in all his life. They said
20 goodbye and Fred ¹turned round to go.
    Suddenly the smile froze on his lips. There, right in front of him,
was Monica!
    'My God! How did SHE manage to ¹turn up here?' he thought,
wishing that at that moment he had been ²turned into a speck of dust
25 and had been blown away by the wind.
    * slang.

QUESTIONS

Complete the answers. Use the words from the story.
1 Which girl did Fred *like very very much*?
  The pretty one sitting outside the cafe turned him . . . . . . (line 6)
2 Why did Fred think she would *refuse* his offer to take her out?
  He thought she would turn him . . . . . because he had been turned
  . . . . . by so many girls. (line 7)
3 Did he ask her straight away or did he *think about it first*?
  He turned it . . . . . . before he decided to try. (line 9)
4 Why didn't he *switch off* the radio?
  He forgot to turn it . . . . . . (line 10)
5 When did Fred *suddenly become* very charming?
  He turned . . . . . . the charm when he spoke to the two girls.
  (line 12)
6 Who wanted to *go to bed* early that night?
  Susan said she wanted to turn . . . . . . early. (line 17)
7 Who *suddenly arrived* unexpectedly?
  Monica turned . . . . . . (line 23)
8 Why did Fred wish he had been *changed into* a speck of dust?
  He wished he had been turned . . . . . . a speck of dust because
  he wanted to escape. (line 24)

EXERCISES

1 TURN INTO
  Example: Fred wished he had *turned into* a speck of dust.
  Passive: Fred wished he had been TURNED into a speck of dust.

  Finish these sentences. The first one has been done for you as an
  example:
  In a paper-mill wood is turned into paper.

In a perfume factory, flowers are turned into . . . .
In a tannery, animal skins . . . .
In a wine factory, grapes . . . .
In an ice works, water . . . .
In a dairy, milk . . . .

Now read your sentences using 'made into' instead of 'turned into'.

2 STRESS PRACTICE

Listen and repeat:
He's turned off the RADIO.
He's turned the RADIO off.
He's turned it OFF.
The radio has been turned OFF.
The offer has been turned DOWN.

3 TURN OFF/TURN ON/TURN UP/TURN DOWN
Example: Fred hasn't *turned* the radio *off.*
Passive: The radio hasn't been turned OFF.

The sentences in A tell you what has happened in the house while
Mr and Mrs Pearson have been out. The sentences in B are Mr
and Mrs Pearson's conclusions about the burglar. **Put a suitable
sentence from B after each of the sentences in A.**

A. *What had happened:*
The TV has been turned on.
The water heater has been turned up.
The electric blanket has been turned on.
The heaters have been turned down.
All the lights have been turned on.
The frig has been turned off.
The oven has been turned on.

B. *Conclusions about the burglar:*
He must have had a bath.
He must have been watching TV.
He must have felt too hot.
He must have wanted to cook something.
He must have been thinking of going to bed.
He must have been in every room.
He must be mad.

4 TURN DOWN
Example: 'So many girls have *turned* me *down*,' thought Fred.
Passive: 'I've been turned DOWN by so many girls,' he thought.

Finish these sentences using 'turn down':

Example: He applied for the job but they . . . . . .
Answer: He applied for the job but they turned him down.

Joe applied for the job but they . . . . . .
Peter offered to help but we . . . . . .
Joe asked Mary to marry him but she . . . . . .
I applied for the job but they . . . . . .
Peter wanted to take Mary to the dance but she . . . . . .

Example: He offered the job to me but I . . . . . .
Answer: He offered the job to me but I turned it down.

We offered the job to Mr Smith but he . . . . . .
I had a very good idea but they . . . . . .
If they offer you the job will you . . . . . . ?
He made some good suggestions but they . . . . . .
We voted Tom president but he . . . . . .

5 TURN OVER
Example: Fred *turned* the idea *over* a few times.

Make sentences from this table:

We really ought to		the suggestion			for a day or two.
Why don't you		the plan			and then decide.
I think I'll	turn	the idea	over		a few times.
You should		it			a bit.
You'd better					

Example:
I think I'll turn the idea over for a day or two.

6 TURN ON
Example: 'That one really *turns* me *on*!' thought Fred.
Passive: Fred was really turned ON by that one.

This is slang, and is only used for some things:
music (a new pop record, for example); a member of the opposite
sex; clothes.

7 TURN ON
Example: Fred *turned on* the charm.

This expression is only used for: the charm; the sarcasm; the tears.
It suggests that the person who did this was not being natural.

8 STRESS PRACTICE

Listen and repeat:
The men ran AWAY.
The money ran OUT.
I'm going to turn IN.
Monica suddenly turned UP.

9 TURN UP
Example: 'How did she manage to *turn up* here?' thought Fred.
Make sentences from this table:

The police			suddenly.
Mary			unexpectedly.
Some uninvited guests	turned up		too late.
His wife			at ten o'clock.
A lot of people			in the middle of the party.
Tom always			when everybody had gone.

Example: The police turned up when everybody had gone.

10 TURN IN
Example: 'I'm going to *turn in* early tonight,' said Susan.
Ask somebody these questions:
When do you usually turn in?
Did you turn in late last night?
Are you going to turn in early tonight?

TEST

A **Fill in the spaces in this story:**
Last Sunday evening Green turned . . . . . . unexpectedly. I really can't
put up with Green, but my wife always feels sorry for him. So I
turned . . . . . . the charm and invited him in. The radio was playing
very quietly, and he immediately turned it . . . . . . loud, then turned
. . . . . . me and said, 'Ah! Doesn't this music turn you . . . . . . ? Let's
have a party.' I turned . . . . . . and ignored his stupid suggestion. I
didn't even turn it . . . . . . in my mind.
    'No? You always turn . . . . . . my best ideas,' he complained.
    'As a matter of fact,' I said rudely, 'We were just going to turn
. . . . . . early when you turned . . . . . .'

B **Write these sentences again in the passive:**
Example: Tom had turned off the radio.
Answer: The radio had been turned off.

1 He hadn't turned the tap off.
2 They have turned down our suggestions.
3 That sort of music has never turned me on.
4 Since he went to that new school Peter has turned into an excellent student.
5 Every girl he asks out turns him down.

C Use one of the verbs you practised in this unit to make a remark that could follow each of these in a conversation:

Example: That music is too loud.
Possible answers: Why don't you turn it down?
But I've already turned it down etc.

1 When did Tom arrive at the party?
2 When do you usually go to bed?
3 This music is marvellous! Do you like it?
4 Did the manager give you the job you asked for?
5 When Tom asked Mary to marry him did she accept?

Unit 9 – to break

It's the men who ³break marriages up.
It's the men who break them up.
It's the men who break up all of them.

The story so far: Fred goes to Brighton for a holiday in order to escape from his fiancée, Monica. He has made friends with two girls, Jeanette and Susan, and has just arranged to take Jeanette out to the cinema when Monica suddenly turns up.

CAPTURED AGAIN

Fred felt like a burglar who has ²broken into a palace only to find it empty; he felt like a man who has ²broken out of prison only to be captured again: he had never felt so disappointed in all his life.
   Monica was so angry she didn't even look at him.
5   'I'm terribly sorry to ²break into this friendly little group,' she said sarcastically to Susan and Jeanette. 'Do let me introduce myself. I'm Fred's fiancée.'
   No one spoke for a moment, and then all at once Susan burst out laughing, and Jeanette surprised everyone by ²breaking into tears.

10   'Monica,' said Fred quietly, 'I think you should . . .'

But Monica ¹broke in as soon as he started speaking. 'Don't tell me
what I should do!' she shouted. 'You promise to marry me. Then you
come here and enjoy yourself with other girls! Spending all that money
that we need for the wedding! You men are all the same! That's how
15 my parents' marriage was ³broken up. It's the men who break them up.
It's the men who break up all of them! The next thing, I suppose you'll
be ³breaking off our engagement, and . . .' She ¹broke off to take out
her handkerchief. '. . . breaking it off . . . and . . . and . . . Oh, Fred!'

Monica couldn't speak any more. She ¹broke down completely, sat
20 down, and cried very, very loudly.

'I think we'd better go,' whispered Susan, and she and Jeanette
quietly disappeared, leaving Fred to comfort his fiancée.

QUESTIONS

Complete the answers. Use the words from the story.
1 Had Fred *forced his way into* a building?
  No. But he felt like a burglar who has broken . . . . . . an empty
  palace. (line 1)
2 Had Fred *forced his way out of* prison?
  No. But he felt like a man who has broken . . . . prison.
  (line 2)
3 Who was sorry to *interrupt* the group of friends?
  Monica said she was sorry to break . . . . . . the group. (line 5)
4 Who *suddenly started* crying?
  Jeanette broke . . . . . . tears. (line 9)
5 *When Fred started speaking* how soon did Monica *interrupt him*?
  She broke . . . . . . as soon as he started speaking. (line 11)
6 Whose marriage *ended in divorce*?
  Monica's parents' marriage broke . . . . . . (line 15)
7 Did Fred *finish their engagement*?
  No. But Monica was afraid he would break it . . . . . . (line 17)
8 Why did Monica *stop speaking suddenly*?
  She broke . . . . . . to take out her handkerchief. (line 17)
9 What did Monica do when she *lost all her self control and
  confidence*?
  When she broke . . . . . . she cried very loudly. (line 19)

EXERCISES

1 STRESS PRACTICE

Listen and repeat:
A: What about (**x**) *the lights?* Did you *switch* them OFF?
B: I switched off (**y**) ALL *of them.*

Note: You can also say: I switched all of them OFF. But, 'I switched off ALL of them', is for emphasis, meaning not just some of them.

Now practise the dialogue above.

(x) Substitute:	(x) Substitute:
the heaters . . . . . . turn down	ALL of them
your friends . . . . . . phone up	MOST of them
the taps . . . . . . turn off	a LOT of them
the lights . . . . . . turn on	SOME of them
these bills . . . . . . run up	a FEW of them

2 BREAK UP

Example i: Monica's parents' marriage *broke up.*

Cue: quarrelled

Response: They *quarrelled* so much that the marriage broke up.

Now give the responses to the following cues.

disagreed / fell out / argued / quarrelled / the family / the two friends / the meeting / the party

Example ii: 'It's the men who *break* marriages *up,*' said Monica.
Passive: Marriages are broken up by men.

DIALOGUE PRACTICE:

A: Do you think many (x)*marriages* have been broken up by(y) *jealousy?*

B That's what broke up (z)*some of them.*

(x) Substitute:	(y) Substitute:	(z) Substitute:
marriages	jealousy	some of them
friendships	arguments	a few of them
families	selfishness	ours
love affairs	quarrelling	theirs
parties	drunkenness	yours
meetings	disagreements	that one / this one

3 BREAK INTO

Example: Fred felt like a burglar who has *broken into* an empty palace.

Passive: The palace has been BROKEN into by a burglar.

Cue: Two men.

Response: Two *men* broke into the house.

Now give the responses to the following cues.

some thieves / a burglar / a thief / you / the bank / the safe / the shop / my money box

4 BREAK OFF
Example: Monica *broke off* to take out her handkerchief.

Cue: I broke off writing to fill my pen.
Response: I was writing, but I broke off to fill my pen.

Now give the responses to the following cues.
He broke off speaking to answer the phone.
The child broke off crying to eat his sweet.
He broke off shouting to listen to the radio.
She broke off speaking to drink her tea.
We broke off talking to watch TV.
They broke off work to have their lunch.

5 BREAK DOWN
Example: Monica *broke down* completely and cried very loudly.
People break down mentally, e.g: He broke down and cried.

Mechanical things break down too.
Example: The car has broken down, so we'll have to go by bus.

Make sentences beginning in the same way about:
the TV / the radio / the telephone / the bus / the train / the clock / the iron / the washing machine

6 BREAK OUT / BREAK INTO
Example: Jeanette surprised everyone by *breaking into* tears.

Make sentences from this table:

Everyone suddenly	broke out	singing.
I asked him why he	burst out	laughing.
I was surprised when he		crying.
She stood up and	broke into	song.
All at once they	burst into	laughter.
Without warning, he		tears.

Example: Everyone suddenly burst out laughing.

7 BREAK IN
Example: Monica *broke in* as soon as he started speaking.
DIALOGUE PRACTICE

Practise reading this dialogue in a group of three people:
Bill: I was telling everybody about it when Tom suddenly broke in and started to talk about . . .
John: Tom's always breaking into other people's conversations.
Bill: As I was saying, he . . .

64

John:	Here he comes! Change the subject. As I was saying, the weather's been very cold and . . .
Tom:	Hello. Sorry to break in, but I must tell you about . . .
Bill:	Oh, shut up! You're always breaking in!

TEST

A Fill in the spaces in this story:

I was very young when *war broke out, but I can remember that day very clearly. My father was shouting at me when he suddenly broke . . . . . . to listen to the radio. The announcer was saying, 'We apologize for breaking . . . . . . this programme. Here is an important announcement: War against Burdania has been declared, and . . .'

At this unfortunate moment our radio broke . . . . . . and my father surprised me by breaking . . . . . . tears. I burst . . . . . . laughing. I was too young to understand the situation, and I had never seen my father break . . . . . .

* war ¹broke out = war began.

B Replace the words in italics by the words in brackets. Give two answers wherever possible.

Example: He made *the story* up. (all of it)
Answer:　He made all of it up.
　　　　　He made up all of it. (Emphatic, meaning not just some of it)

1 He turned *the invitations* down. (all of them)
2 Please turn *the lights* on. (some of them)
3 Please turn *the light* on. (it)
4 I put *my coat* on. (mine)
5 I can't make out *your writing*. (yours)

C Use one of the verbs you practised in this unit to make a remark that could follow each of these in a conversation:

Example: Why did he suddenly stop speaking?
Possible answers: He broke off to answer the phone.
　　　　　　　　　He broke off to speak to somebody else, etc.

1 Did you walk here? What's happened to your car?
2 Did you say Tom and Mary were divorced? What happened?
3 What did she do when she heard that her parents were dead?
4 What did Jane do when she heard that her fiancé was going out with another girl?
5 Look! There's a strange man trying to open the window of the neighbours' house. What do you think he's doing?

Unit 10 – to get

I have to ¹get out.
I have to ²get out of the car.

The story so far: Fred has gone to Brighton for a holiday in order to escape from his fiancée, Monica. Monica follows him to Brighton, and is very angry and upset when she finds him with two other girls.

TROUBLE GETTING BACK

Fred and Monica stayed the night in Brighton, and Monica ²got over the shock of finding him with two other girls. But she insisted that they should ¹get back the next day, and that they should ¹get up early and hitch-hike home to save money. Fred was worried. 'We might ²get into
5 trouble,' he said. But Monica insisted.
　　The next morning Fred went to the reception desk to ³get his money back. He had paid two weeks in advance for his room, and to his surprise the manager tried to ²get out of returning the money. Fred didn't know what to do, so he went to Monica, who was busy packing
10 his suitcase.
　　'That's robbery!' she said. 'Don't let him ²get away with it. Go back

and shout at him. And let me ²get on with my packing.'

The manager had been very rude before, but when Fred shouted at him he became extremely friendly and gave the money back straight away.

'That's strange,' thought Fred. 'He was very friendly to me. Perhaps I'd ²get on with people better if I shouted more often!'

They ²got away from the hotel very quickly and stood on the side of the road waiting to be picked up. It wasn't long before a car stopped.

'¹Get in!' shouted the driver cheerfully. They were pleased to get a lift so quickly, but they soon realized why the driver was so cheerful. He was drunk, and he was driving very dangerously.

How could they ²get out of the car? Monica thought quickly, then, 'Please stop. I have to ¹get out. I'm going to be sick!' she said. Those were the last words that Fred heard. The only other thing he remembered was the tremendous crash as the driver braked suddenly and a car ran into the back of them. When he came to, he was lying in a hospital bed and a beautiful nurse was leaning over him.

QUESTIONS

1 What shock did Monica *recover from*?
She got . . . . . . the shock of finding him with two other girls. (line 1)

2 When did they decide to *return* home?
They decided to get . . . . . . the next day. (line 3)

3 When did they *get out of bed*?
They got . . . . . . very early. (line 3)

4 Who thought they might *be involved in some trouble* if they hitch-hiked?
Fred thought they might get . . . . . . trouble. (line 4)

5 Where did Fred go *to have his money returned*?
He went to the reception desk to get it . . . . . . (line 6)

6 Who tried *to avoid doing something he should do*?
The manager tried to get . . . . returning Fred's money. (line 8)

7 Who wouldn't let the manager *succeed in doing something wrong*?
Monica wouldn't let him get . . . . it. (line 11)

8 Who wanted *to continue with her job of* packing?
Monica wanted to get . . . . it. (line 12)

9 How does Fred think he can *have a good relationship with people*?
He thinks he can get . . . . people better if he shouts more. (line 17)

10 How soon did they *escape from* the hotel?
They got . . . . the hotel very quickly. (line 18)

EXERCISES

1 GET OVER

    Example: Monica got over the shock of finding him with two other
                girls.

    Cue: surprise.
    Response: He soon got over the *surprise.*

Now give the responses to the following cues.
illness / operation / insult / accident / gradually / quickly / never /
slowly

2 STRESS PRACTICE

Listen and repeat:

I have to get OUT.
I have to get OUT of the CAR.
They got AWAY.
They got AWAY from the HOTEL.
We don't get ON.
I don't get ON with him very well.

Note: These can be Pattern 1 or Pattern 2 (ii) Verbs without any
change in meaning.

3 GET OUT/IN
    GET AWAY

    Examples: 'I have to *get out*.'
                  'I have to *get out of* the car.'
                  They *got away* very quickly.
                  They *got away from* the hotel very quickly.

    Cue: I've lost my key, and I can't get in. (the house)
    Response: I've lost my key, and I can't get into the house.
    Cue: I wanted to get away. (that noisy party)
    Response: I wanted to get away from that noisy party.

Now give the responses to these cues.
The burglars tried to get in. (the building)
The burglars got away. (the police)
Open the door, please. I want to get out. (the car)
The door stuck, and we couldn't get out. (the lift)
I thought we'd never get away. (that boring man)
It's difficult to get away. (him)
There's going to be a fight soon. Let's get out. (this place)
Get out, and never come back! (this house)

4 GET BACK

Example: They decided to *get back* the next day.·
They decided to *get back* to Folkestone the next day.
Cue: to a hot meal.
Response: Let's get back *to a hot meal.*

Now give the responses to these cues.

to a warm fire/to a comfortable chair/to Folkestone/to my place/
home / and relax / and have something to eat / and go to bed /

5 GET ON

Example: 'We'd *get on* better.'
'I'd *get on with* people better.'

DIALOGUE PRACTICE

i.

A: How do (x) *you* get on with *your neighbours?*

B: I don't get on / get on with them very well.

(x) Substitute:

you . . . . . your parents	the Pearsons . . . . . . the Dobsons
you . . . . . your teachers	Tom . . . . . . his secretary
you . . . . . Mary	Mary . . . . . her boss

ii.

Now practise these answers to the same questions:

We | don't get on
They | get on   very well.

6 STRESS PRACTICE

Listen and repeat:

He tried to get OUT of it.
Don't let him get AWAY with it.
Let me get ON with it.

Note: These cannot be Pattern 1 Verbs without a change in meaning.
Example: He tried to ¹get out. (Meaning that he was locked in a
room, for example.)

7 GET ON WITH

Example: 'Let me *get on with* my packing,' said Monica.

Cue: a party . . . . . English
Response A: Would you like to come to *a party*?
B: I'd love to, but I have to get on with my *English*.

the park . . . . . . work	a dance . . . . . . studying
the theatre . . . . . . reading	a pub . . . . . . homework
the cinema . . . . . . sewing	a discothèque . . . . . . English

8 GET OUT OF

Example: The manager tried to *get out of* returning Fred's money.

Make sentences from this table:

My brother		doing the work	by pretending to be ill.
Mary		the work	by hiding somewhere.
My friend	gets out of	washing up	by going out.
My sister		making the tea	by pretending to be busy.
Tom		cooking breakfast	by going to the toilet.

Example: My brother gets out of cooking breakfast by pretending to be busy.

9 GET AWAY WITH

Example: 'Don't let him *get away with* it,' said Monica.

DIALOGUE PRACTICE

A: Jim always (**x**) *arrives late for work.*
B: Doesn't he get into trouble?
A: No, he doesn't. He always gets away with it.

(x) Substitute:

arrives late for class
parks his car illegally
travels without a ticket

forgets to do his homework
steals books from the library
drives through red lights

TEST

A Fill in the spaces in this story:

Bill was working with me till he got the sack. I /got . . . .
him very well, even though he tried to get . . . . doing the
jobs he didn't like. He usually got . . . . it too. Then one
day Mr Smith, the boss, had gone out. I was getting . . . .
the work, but Bill was sitting down smoking a cigarette.

'You'll get . . . . . . trouble,' I said. Bill just laughed.

'And you'll *get on,' he said. 'I can just see you sitting behind old
Smithey's desk!'

Just at that moment 'old Smithey' walked in. He had got . . . . . .
earlier than we expected. The thing was, I had lent Bill five pounds the
day before, and I never did get it . . . . . .

* You'll ¹get on = You'll make progress in your work, get promotion.

B Finish these sentences with the words in brackets:

Example: Do you want to get out? (the car)
Answer: Do you want to get out of the car?

1 Do you want to get in? (the car)
2 We finally got away. (that boring man)
3 The men ran away. (the police)
4 They don't get on. (their parents)
5 Have you run out? (money)

C Use the verbs you practised in this unit to make a remark that could follow each of these in a conversation:

Example: Shall I steal this book?
Possible Answers: No. You won't get away with it.
You'll get into trouble, etc.

1 Jim stole a book, but they didn't catch him.
2 Does your husband do the washing up?
3 Why can't you come out for lunch?
4 Are Mr Jones and his secretary on friendly terms?
5 Why are they knocking on the door?

Unit 11 – to look

Fred [1]looked up.
Fred [2]looked up to the nurses.

The story so far: When Fred goes to Brighton for a holiday to escape from his fiancée, Monica, she follows him. She insists that they hitch-hike home to save money, and on the way home they are involved in a car accident.

FRED IN HOSPITAL

After the accident Fred and Monica were taken to Brighton Hospital. Monica had only minor injuries, and she was allowed to go home after a few days. But Fred was seriously injured.

Fred was [2]looked after very well in the hospital. He admired the
5 nurses and [2]looked up to them, thinking how hard they worked. Nurse Johnson was the kindest one, and he really [2]looked on her as a mother, she was so good to him.

Poor Fred lay on his back for weeks, and he had plenty of time to
[2]look back on the past and think about the times he had spent with
10 Monica. He got letters from George and Molly, and of course from

Monica too, but none of them had much time to come and ³look him up, they were so busy and Brighton so far away.

Fred's window ²looked onto the street, and every afternoon he would ²look for Monica's face among the crowd of visitors arriving at the
15 front gate. Of course she usually didn't come, and then he could only ¹look on sadly while the other patients talked so happily with their friends. He was really ²looking forward to seeing Monica again!

QUESTIONS

Complete the answers. Use the words from the story.

1 Fred was *nursed and taken care of* very well in the hospital, wasn't he?
Yes. He was looked . . . . . . very well. (line 4)

2 Why did Fred *respect* the nurses so much?
He looked . . . . them because they worked so hard. (line 5)

3 Why did Fred *think of* Nurse Johnson *as* a mother?
He looked . . . . . . her as a mother because she was so kind. (line 6)

4 Who had plenty of time *to remember and think about the past?*
Fred had plenty of time to look . . . . the past. (line 9)

5 Why didn't Fred's friends come and *visit* him often?
They were too busy to look him . . . . . . (line 11)

6 Fred's window *had a view of* the street, didn't it?
Yes. His window looked . . . . . . the street. (line 13)

7 Whose face was Fred *trying to find* among the crowd of visitors?
He was looking . . . . . . Monica's face. (line 14)

8 Who *watched but couldn't do anything* while the other patients talked to their friends?
Fred looked . . . . . . (line 16)

9 Fred was unhappy in hospital, but he was *thinking of the future and thinking how he was going to enjoy* seeing Monica again, wasn't he?
Yes. He was looking . . . . seeing Monica again. (line 17)

EXERCISES

1 STRESS AND PRACTICE

Listen and repeat:
Fred looked UP to the NURSES.
He looked UP to them.
He looked BACK on the PAST.
He looked BACK on it.
He was looking FORWARD to SEEING her.
He was looking FORWARD to it.
Note: These cannot be Pattern 1 Verbs without a change in meaning.

2 LOOK UP TO

Example: Fred *looked up to* the nurses.

Cue: are rich

Response   *Student A:* Do you look up to people who are rich?

             Student B: Yes, I do.

                             No, I don't.

Are clever / work hard / are older than you / are stronger than you / wear expensive clothes / are good at sports / have big cars / come from a rich family

Note: 'He ¹looked up' means just:

3 LOOK BACK ON
Example: Fred *looked back on* the past.

DIALOGUE PRACTICE

A: Do you	sometimes ever often like to	look back on	the good old days? the past? your childhood? your schooldays?

B: Yes, I do.
    No, I don't.

4 LOOK FORWARD TO
Example: Fred was really *looking forward to* seeing Monica again.

Cue: the party.

Response: I'm looking forward to *the party.*

Now give the responses to these cues.

the holidays / the weekend / Saturday night / having a party / going away / seeing you again / hearing from you

5 LOOK ON . . . AS
Example: Fred *looked on* Nurse Johnson *as* a mother.

DIALOGUE PRACTICE:

A: Do you consider Tom a **(x)** *friendly person?*

B: Yes. I've always looked on him as a very *friendly person.*

(x) Substitute:

generous person / selfish person / hard worker / honest man / intelligent man / safe driver

6 LOOK ONTO

Example: Fred's window *looked onto* the street.

What does your
| classroom |
| bedroom |
| kitchen |
| sitting room |
window look onto?

7 LOOK AFTER

Example: The nurses *looked after* Fred very well.
Passive: Fred was LOOKED after very well.
  OR   Fred was looked AFTER very well.

Cue: your little brother
Response Student A: You'll have to look after *your little brother.*
  Student B: But I haven't got time to look after him.

Now give the response to the following cues.

your little sister / the baby / the children / Grandma / the dog / Grandad / the house / the garden / the shop / the business

You can also look after: a farm, a car, your books, your shoes, your hair, your teeth, your appearance, your clothes, your health, yourself.

Write sentences about two of these.

8 LOOK ON

Fred *looked on* sadly while the other patients talked.

Complete the sentences in A with a suitable ending taken from B.
A.
The medical students looked on . . . . . .
He looked on, but because he was ill . . . . . .
That lazy boy just looks on while . . . . . .
The hitch-hikers looked on . . . . . .
I don't like people who just look on . . . . . .
B.
he couldn't help.
and criticize my work.
while I changed the wheel.
the others do the work.
while the surgeon operated.

9 LOOK UP

Example: None of his friends had time to *look* him *up*.

i. DIALOGUE PRACTICE

A: Why don't you look (x) *the Clarks* up?

B: I'm going to look them up (y) *one day soon.*

(x) Substitute:

the Dobsons
Aunt Mary
us
me
your old friends

(y) Substitute:

one of these days
after my exams
on my way to Paris
when I go to Scotland
one day next week

You can also look up information in a book:

ii. DIALOGUE PRACTICE

A: Did you look up *that phone number*? (Or did you look that phone number up?)

B: Yes. I looked it up in *a telephone directory.*

(x) Substitute:

that word . . . . . . a dictionary
the information . . . . . . an encyclopædia
the train time . . . . . . a time table
the recipe . . . . . . a cookery book
the name of the street . . . . . . a street directory
the name of the country . . . . . . an atlas

TEST

A Fill in the spaces in this story:

My mother looked . . . . . . Johnny as one of the family, and she always looked . . . . his visits. He sometimes looked . . . . . . the baby while she went shopping. Her sitting room window looked . . . . . . the street, and she would often see Johnny being teased by the other children. They all *looked down on him because his father was very poor. My mother looked . . . . . . , but there was nothing she could do to help. Most people look . . . . their childhood with pleasure. I wonder if Johnny does.

*to ²look down on someone is the opposite of 'to look up to someone'.

B Complete this dialogue using the words in brackets:

1 A: I can't find my address book.

1 B: . . . . ? (up)

  A: Mary Smith's. We're going to her party tonight.

2 B: . . . . ? (after)

  A: We've arranged for a baby sitter to come.

3 B: . . . . ? (forward to)

  A: Oh, yes. It's going to be a wonderful party.

C Use the verbs you practised in this unit to make a remark that could follow each of these in a conversation:

Example: His car is always very clean.

Possible Answers: Yes. He always looks after his car.
His wife looks after it for him, etc.

1 I don't know how to spell that word.
2 Has your new house got a good view?
3 Do you remember the good times we had on that holiday?
4 You say you brother is coming home next week. You haven't seen him for a long time, have you?
5 My cousin lives very close to where you're going for your holiday. Here's his address.

Unit 12 – to take

He [3]took his pullovers off.
He took them off.
He took off both of them.

The story so far: Fred has been in hospital for a long time as a result of a car accident. While in hospital he finds that he really misses his fiancée, Monica, very much. This is surprising because he didn't want to get married, and was always trying to escape from her.

FRED COMES OUT OF HOSPITAL

Fred [3]took up basket-making in hospital, and by the time he got out he had made a lot of baskets.

When he got back to Folkestone he took a taxi straight to Monica's house. He [3]took up a lot of space in the taxi with his crutches; it was a 5 hot day and he was wearing two pullovers, but he managed to [3]take off both of them. It was a very uncomfortable journey.

As the taxi turned into Monica's street, Fred was surprised to see a very large, expensive car [1]taking off at high speed from Monica's house. And he was completely [3]taken aback to see Monica sitting

10 beside the driver, a rather handsome, older man. Monica didn't see Fred. She was looking at the other man and they were laughing together.

Fred quietly told the taxi driver to turn round, but he was thinking angrily as the taxi made for his house: 'There I was lying in hospital,
15 and she's ²taken up with some rich old *sugar daddy! What does she ³take me for? An idiot? He must be very rich. He's probably ³taken her in with all his money—³taking her out to expensive restaurants and night-clubs. If I weren't on crutches I'd have ³taken him on straight away! I'd have taken on both of them!'

20 Fred was very jealous. Even when he got home he still couldn't stop thinking about Monica. 'Oh, yes,' he thought angrily, 'She really ³takes after her mother—always thinking about money. I'll give her a piece of my mind.' Then without thinking twice about it he picked up the phone and dialled Monica's number. Monica's mother answered.
25 'Mrs Brown? Is that you . . . ?'

'Fred! You're out of hospital! How lovely! We . . . er . . . we have a surprise for you. Monica wants to introduce you to somebody very nice. She ²took to him straight away. He's very rich, and he . . . Fred? Fred?'
30 But Fred had hung up.

* slang, meaning a rich man who is much older than his girl friend.

QUESTIONS

Complete the answers. Use the words from the story.
1 What *hobby* did Fred *start* while he was in hospital?
He took . . . . . . basket making. (line 1)
2 Why did Fred *occupy* a lot of space in the taxi?
He took . . . . . . a lot of space because of his crutches. (line 4)
3 Did he put on two pullovers in the taxi?
No. He took them . . . . . . (line 5)
4 Where was the expensive car *leaving very quickly* from?
It was taking . . . . . . from Monica's house. (line 8)
5 Who was *very surprised* to see Monica in the expensive car?
Fred was taken . . . . . . (line 9)
6 What *unsuitable friendship* does Fred think that Monica had *formed* while he was in hospital?
She had taken . . . . a rich man who was much older than her. (line 15)
7 Does Monica *mistakenly think that* Fred *is an* idiot?
Fred thinks that Monica takes him . . . . . . an idiot. (line 16)
8 How does Fred think that the rich man had *deceived and tricked* Monica?
Fred thinks he's taken her . . . . . . with all his money. (line 16)

9 Why didn't Fred *fight* the other man?
   He didn't take him . . . . . . because he was on crutches. (line 18)
10 Fred thought Monica *resembled one of her parents*—which one?
   She took . . . . . . her mother. (line 21)
11 Who *liked* the rich man *as soon as they met?*
   Monica took . . . . . . him straight away. (line 28)

EXERCISES

1 STRESS PRACTICE

Cue:	Response:
Did he take ONE of his pullovers off?	No. He took off BOTH of them.
Did he take BOTH of his pullovers off?	No. He took off ONE of them.

Did Tom take BOTH of the girls out?
Did Peter take ONE of his socks off?
Did Mary take BOTH her gloves off?
Did you take ONE of these library books out?
Did you take ONE of your friends out?

2 TAKE UP

Example: He *took up* a lot of space in the taxi with his crutches.
Passive: A lot of space was taken UP by Fred's crutches.

Cue:	Response:
Does studying take up a lot of your time?	It takes up all of it.
Does cooking take up all of your time?	It takes up a lot of it.

Now give the responses to these cues.
Does learning English take up a lot of your time?
Does coming to English class take up all of your free time?
Does that car take up a lot of space in your garage?
Does that picture take up all the space on your wall?
Will a swimming pool take up only a little space in the garden?
Will a piano take up only a little space in the sitting room?

3 TAKE UP

Example: Fred *took up* basket-making in hospital.

DIALOGUE PRACTICE:

A: What hobby do you go in for?
          sport

B: I go in for . . . . . .

A: When   did you take it up?
   How long ago

B: I took it up . . . . . .

4 TAKE IN

Example: He's probably *taken* her *in* with all his money.
Passive: She's probably been taken IN.

DIALOGUE PRACTICE:
A: I didn't realize at first that Smith was **(x)** *a liar*.
B: Why did you trust him? Everyone knows he's *a liar*.
A: I was taken in by his **(y)** *charming manner*.

(x) Substitute:	**(y) Substitute:**
a thief	friendly manner
a cheat	generosity
a rogue	innocent smile
dishonest	appearance
lying	lies

5 TAKE ABACK

Example: Fred was *taken aback* to see Monica sitting beside the driver.
Passive: This expression is nearly always passive.

Cue: drunk
Response *Student A:* George is drunk.

Student B: Good heavens!
        gracious!

Student C: Were you surprised to hear that George was *drunk?*

Student B: I was completely taken aback when A told me.
                        I heard about it.

Now give the responses to the following cues.
engaged / married / a father / a grandfather / seriously ill / dead

6 TAKE FOR

Example: 'What does she *take* me *for*? An idiot?' thought Fred.
Passive: He was TAKEN for an idiot.

Cue: teacher . . . student
Response *Student A:* He's a teacher, isn't he?
        Student B: No. He's a student.
        Student A: I took him for a teacher.

Now give the responses to the following cues.

Englishman . . . Frenchman	nurse . . . waitress
doctor . . . patient	film star . . . typist
pop singer . . . politician	student . . . teacher

7 TAKE TO

Example: Monica *took to* him straight away.

i.

Cue: Did you like Mary when you first met?
Response: Yes. I took to her straight away.

Now give the responses to the following cues.
Did you like Susan when you first met?
Did you like Tom when you first met?
Did you like your neighbours when you first met?
Did the neighbours like Mary when they first met?
Did Tom like Mary when they first met?
Did you like me when we first met?

ii.
Now answer the same questions in this way:

Yes. We / They took to each other immediately. / straight away. / right from the start.

8 TAKE AFTER

Example: 'Monica *takes after* her mother,' thought Fred.

Who do you take after—your mother or your father? Write a sentence about this beginning:

I take after my mother / father because we both . . . . . .

9 TAKE OFF

Example: A car was *taking off* at high speed.

This expression is usually for planes. Write a sentence about a plane taking off.

10 TAKE UP WITH

Example: 'She's *taken up with* some rich old sugar daddy!' thought Fred.

This expression suggests that the speaker thinks this is an unsuitable Friendship: e.g. someone too old; too young; too poor; too un-educated.

TEST

A Fill in the spaces in this story:

My father was very mean about money. I take . . . . . . him. So when the price of petrol went up I decided to sell my big old car. It took . . . . . . too much space anyway. I decided to take . . . . . . cycling instead. The salesman in the bicycle shop was extremely helpful, and I bought the most expensive bicycle in the shop. So I was completely taken . . . . . . when it broke down the very next day. I had taken that salesman . . . . . . an honest man, but he had taken me . . . . . . with his helpful manner. When I found this out, I want straight back to the shop, took . . . . . . my coat, and offered to take him . . . . . . My father would have done the same, I'm sure.

B Replace the words in italics by the words in brackets. Give two answers wherever possible.

Example: He took *his pullovers* off. (both of them)
Answer: He took both of them off.
            He took off BOTH of them. (Emphatic—meaning not just one of them.)

1 He took *his shoes* off. (one of them)
2 Studying takes *my time* up. (all of it)
3 I'll take *my gloves* off. (them)
4 Fred got *his money* back. (all of it)
5 Let's take *all our friends* out for a meal. (them)

C Use the verbs you practised in this unit to make a remark that could follow each of these in a conversation:

Example: Did you like your best friend when you first met?
Possible Answers: Yes. We took to each other immediately.
            No. We didn't take to each other at first, etc.

1 Do I look like my mother?
2 Was Bill very surprised when you told him about it?
3 What time does your plane leave?
4 When did you first start playing tennis?
5 Oh! My feet are sore! These shoes are too tight.

Review – Units 7-12

'Wh' Questions Quiz

Unit 7

1 Which batteries were run DOWN?
2 How many people were run DOWN?
3 What had Fred run OUT of?
4 Who did Fred run INTO in the pub?
5 Who ran AWAY from the police?

Unit 8

6 When is Susan going to turn IN?
7 Who suddenly turned UP?
8 What did Fred wish he could be turned INTO?

Unit 9

9 Whose marriage had broken UP?
10 Who broke DOWN?

Unit 10

11 What did Monica get OVER?
12 What did Fred get BACK?
13 What did the hotel manager try to get OUT of?
14 What did Monica want to get ON with?

Unit 11

15 Who did the nurses look AFTER?
16 Who did Fred look UP to?
17 What did Fred's window look ONTO?
18 What did Fred look BACK on?
19 What was Fred Looking FORWARD to?

Unit 12

20 What hobby did Fred take UP?
21 How many pullovers did he take OFF?
22 If he hadn't been on crutches, who would Fred have taken ON?
23 Who did Fred think that Monica had taken UP with?
24 Who does Monica take AFTER?

Unit 13 - Review

It ¹kept on ringing.
It kept on.
I'll ²go in for hunting.
I'll go in for it.
I'll ³take up shooting.
I'll take it up.

The story so far: Fred has just been in hospital for a long time. When he comes out he sees his fiancée, Monica, with a handsome, older man in an expensive car. He is very jealous. He phones up Monica's mother, but when she starts to talk about the rich man Monica wants to introduce him to, he hangs up.

THE END

Fred couldn't decide what to do. He was ²looking forward to telling Monica exactly what he thought of her, but at the same time he wanted to ³put off speaking to her for as long as possible. So he didn't answer the telephone, even though it ¹kept on ringing for a very long time.

5 Instead he ¹went on day-dreaming about what he would do to Monica's new boy friend.

'I'll ³take up shooting,' he thought. 'I don't even know how to hold a gun, but I'll ²go in for hunting like George and get as much practice as I can. I'll even ³give up drinking to keep my hand steady. I'll . . .'

10 Fred suddenly ¹broke off day-dreaming and listened. Somebody was knocking loudly on his door. Fred opened it without thinking. Standing in the doorway were Monica, her mother, and the man with the expensive car.

'This is my fiancé,' said Monica's mother proudly, 'your future

15 father-in-law!'

'And he's going to buy us a super new house!' shouted Monica excitedly.

'Just call me Bert,' said the owner of the expensive car. 'Yes, you can have the house,' he added, 'if you can ²put up with living near us. It's

20 just two streets away. But we can both ²get out of doing the washing-up and ³take up going to pubs together in the evenings!' and he winked at Fred.

Fred thought he was going mad. He sat down, trembling, head in his hands.

25 'I was just ²thinking of killing you,' he whispered to Bert. 'I thought you were Monica's new boy friend.' Bert ¹burst out laughing, and he ¹went on laughing for a very long time. Monica hadn't even heard what Fred had said. She was holding both his hands and talking about their new house, and she ¹kept on talking for a very long time.

EXERCISES

1 **Complete these sentences using 'ing'.**

Example: I can't put up with people . . . . . (tell lies)
I can't put up with people telling lies.

I'm looking forward to . . . . . . (go away on holiday)
Do you go in for . . . . . . ? (swim)
My brother always gets out of . . . . . . (do the housework)
I'm thinking of . . . . . . (buy a car)
My tooth was very sore, but I had to put off . . . . . (go to the dentist's)
You should give up . . . . . . (smoke)
When did you take up . . . . . . ? (ride)
He broke off . . . . . . to answer the phone. (speak)
It was very late, but we went on . . . . . . (walk)
My neighbour keeps on . . . . . . (have noisy parties)
Everyone suddenly burst out . . . . . . (laugh)

2 STRESS PRACTICE

Listen and repeat:

The phone kept on RINGING.
It kept ON.
He went on LAUGHING.
He went ON.
He broke off DAY-DREAMING.
He broke OFF.

3 PATTERN 1 VERBS

Cue: The phone went on ringing for a long time.
Response: Yes, it went on.

Now give the responses to the following cues.

The bell went on ringing for a long time.
He kept on asking till she agreed.
They broke off speaking when we came in.
He gave up trying in the end.
It went on raining.
It went on and on snowing.
She broke off speaking to take out her handkerchief.
They kept on arguing till I told them to be quiet.

4 STRESS PRACTICE

Listen and repeat:

I'll go IN for HUNTING.
I'll go IN for it.
They'll get OUT of WASHING UP.
They'll get OUT of it.
He was looking FORWARD to TELLING her.
He was looking FORWARD to it.

5 PATTERN 2 (ii) VERBS

Cue: He went in for hunting.
Response: Why did he go in for it?

Now give the responses to the following cues.
She went in for flying.
I got out of paying.
I put up with the shouting.
He looked forward to seeing her.
I got out of doing the homework.
We put up with listening to her for hours.
He looked forward to telling her the truth.
They went in for collecting match boxes.

6 STRESS PRACTICE

Listen and repeat:

I'll take up SHOOTING.
I'll take it UP.
I'll give up DRINKING.
I'll give it UP.
I'll put off SPEAKING to her.
I'll put it OFF.

7 PATTERN 3 VERBS

i.

Cue: I've taken up skiing.
Response: Why did you take it up?

Now give the responses to the following cues.

He's taken up mountaineering.
I've given up smoking.
They've put off getting married.
Mary's taken up bowling.
We've put off going away.
Tom's given up drinking.
Peter's given up farming.

ii.

DIALOGUE PRACTICE:

A: Has Tom (x)*given up drinking?*
B: He hasn't given up *drinking*, but he's given up (y)*smoking.*

(x) Substitute	(y) Substitute
given up drinking	gambling
taken up skiing	skating
given up gambling	going to the races
given up smoking.	smoking other people's cigarettes

8 PATTERNS 1, 2(ii) and 3 VERBS

i.

Cue:	*Response:*
He kept on asking me, didn't he?	Yes, he kept on.
Tom's given up smoking, hasn't he?	Yes, he's given it up.
I got out of paying, didn't I?	Yes, you got out of it.
John kept on drinking, didn't he?	
Peter has given up farming, hasn't he?	
You're looking forward to going away, aren't you?	
She suddenly broke off speaking, didn't she?	
They got out of doing the work, didn't they?	

I'll give up smoking one day, won't I?
They've taken up horse riding, haven't they?
We're looking forward to having a break, aren't we?

ii.

DIALOGUE PRACTICE:
A: You should (x)*give up smoking.*
B: But I couldn't possibly give it up.
A: Then you'll have to (y)*give up drinking.*

(x) Substitute:	(y) Substitute:
take up running	take up cycling
go in for swimming	go in for walking
give up drinking	give up going to parties
think of retiring	think of working part time
put up with being fat..........	go in for exercising
put off going out	put off having the Taylors for dinner

TEST

A Fill in the spaces in this story:

It was really the doctor's fault that I got so fat. I had kept ......
coughing very badly, but I put ...... going to the doctor's for as long
as possible. I tried to put .... having no sleep. But when
my mother found out, I couldn't get .... making an
appointment. The doctor told me to give ...... smoking and go
.... exercising. He suggested that I take ......
swimming or walking. I did what he said, and it was to make up for not
smoking that I took to eating so much instead!

B Replace the italicized words by 'it'.

Example: Out neighbour has taken up *gardening.*
Answer: Out neighbour has taken it up.

1 I've given up *smoking.*
2 He goes in for *swimming* very enthusiastically.
3 My brother gets out of *doing the washing-up* by pretending to be ill.
4 I'll take up *skating* next year.
5 Are you looking forward to *going away*?

C Use the verbs you practised in this unit to make a remark that could follow each of these in a conversation. Use the 'ing' form wherever possible.

Example: Did you start any new hobbies last year?
Possible answers: Yes. I took up stamp collecting.
     I took up acting, etc.

1 What sports have you started recently?
2 What do you do in your spare time?
3 You spend so much on cigarettes, how will you save enough money for your holiday?
4 Did you stop the party when the neighbours complained about the noise? (go on)
5 Will you be glad when your exams are finished? (look forward)

ANSWERS TO QUIZ QUESTIONS

REVIEW—UNITS 1-6

1.the alarm clock 2.Fred's 3. Fred 4. Monica 5. food 6. to escape 7. hunting 8. to marry Monica 9. Fred and Monica 10. the light 11. her coat 12. the next visit 13. Monica 14. the vicarage 15. Molly's writing, or the address 16. that their car had broken down, and that one of them was lame 17. Fred's car 18. a book 19. it had just come out 20. the light cord 21. after a few minutes 22. the doctor 23. Fred 24. Fred

REVIEW—UNITS 7-12

1. the batteries of Fred's radio 2. three 3. money 4. George 5. the thieves 6. early 7. Monica 8. a speck of dust 9. Monica's parents' 10. Monica 11. the shock of finding Fred with two other girls 12. his money 13. returning Fred's money 14. the packing 15. Fred 16. the nurses 17. the street 18. the past, or the times he had spent with Monica 19. seeing Monica again 20. basket-making 21. two 22. the older man and Monica 23. a rich sugar daddy 24. her mother